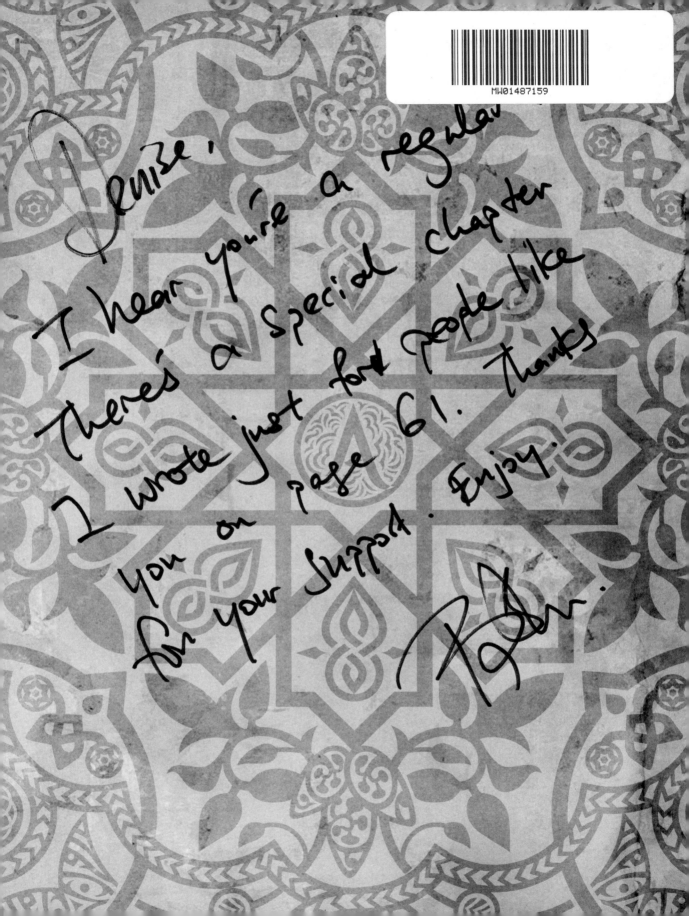

Denise,

I hear you're a regular. There's a special chapter I wrote just for people like you on page 61. Thanks for your support. Enjoy.

artichoke

Edited by Samantha Lee;
designed by Yong Wen Yeu;
Artichoke identity by Shoon Teoh.

National Library Board, Singapore
Cataloguing-in-Publication Data

Shen, Bjorn, 1982-
Artichoke : recipes & stories from
Singapore's most rebellious kitchen
/ Bjorn Shen. Singapore : Epigram
Books, [2014]
pages cm
ISBN: 978-981-07-9773-7 (paperback)
ISBN: 978-981-4615-01-3 (ebook)

1. Artichoke (Restaurant)
2. Restaurants – Singapore.
3. Cooking, Middle Eastern. I. Title.

TX945.4
647.955957-- dc23   OCN 882976804

First Edition
10 9 8 7 6 5 4 3 2 1

**Recipes & Stories from
Singapore's Most Rebellious Kitchen**

BJORN SHEN

Table of Contents

A Forward Foreword 6

Notes from an Artichoke Stalker 8

Part I   Why Write This Book? 10

Part II   How To Use This Book, or How To Rock Out With Your Fork Out 14

Part III   Some Pantry Basics 16

Chapter 1   The Little Place with No Signboard 20

Chapter 2   No Doner Kebabs, No Persian Carpets 34

Chapter 3   Getting Slammed 46

Chapter 4   Managing Customers is Like Playing Mah-jong: A Lesson in Business 60

Chapter 5   What's So Difficult About That? 72

Chapter 6   The Lousy Beetroot Salad 78

Chapter 7   Cuts & Burns 84

Chapter 8   Reckless Creativity 94

Chapter 9   The Lambgasm 114

Chapter 10 People of Artichoke, Past & Present 120

Chapter 11 Tattoos & Tomatoes 136

Chapter 12 Staff Meals 148

Chapter 13 Bacon is Evil, We Must Destroy It with Our Teeth 158

Chapter 14 Nothing Escapes the Fryer 172

Chapter 15 Every Day I Die a Little 182

Chapter 16 Artichoke Abroad 204

Chapter 17 Lolly Bags 222

Chapter 18 Overdoughs 240

Chapter 19 Condiments 252

So You Wanna Hold an Artichoke-style Party? 266

Acknowledgements 268

Index 269

A Forward Foreword

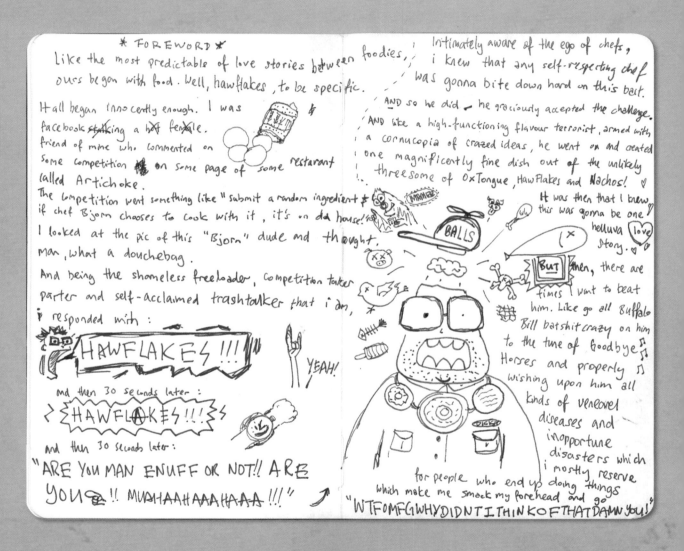

* FOREWORD *

Like the most predictable of love stories between foodies, ours began with food. Well, hawflakes, to be specific.

It all began innocently enough. I was facebook stalking a hot female friend of mine who commented on some competition on some page of some restaurant called Artichoke.

The competition went something like "submit a random ingredient & if chef Bjorn chooses to cook with it, it's on da house!"
I looked at the pic of this "Bjorn" dude and thought, man, what a douchebag.

And being the shameless freeloader, competition taker parter and self-acclaimed trashtalker that i am, i responded with:

HAWFLAKES !!!

and then 30 seconds later: HAWFLAKES !!!

and then 30 seconds later:

"ARE YOU MAN ENUFF OR NOT!! ARE YOU !! MUAHAAHAAAHAAA !!!"

YEAH!

Intimately aware of the ego of chefs, i knew that any self-respecting chef was gonna bite down hard on this bait.
AND so he did — he graciously accepted the challenge.
AND like a high-functioning flavour terrorist, armed with a cornucopia of crazed ideas, he went on and created one magnificently fine dish out of the unlikely threesome of Ox Tongue, Haw Flakes and Nachos!

It was then that I knew this was gonna be one helluva love story.
BUT then, there are times I want to beat him. Like go all Buffalo Bill batshit crazy on him to the tune of goodbye Horses and properly wishing upon him all kinds of venereal diseases and inopportune disasters which i mostly reserve for people who end up doing things which make me smack my forehead and go "WTFOMFGWHYDIDNTITHINKOFTHATDAMNYOU!"

like when he created this mad superfresh salad and topped it with an oldskool childhood crispy ramen snack, Mamee roundhouse kicking your tastebuds with seven shades of u-mamee (pun intended)

Or God knows what went through his mind when he took labneh, added ebiko, topped it with chunks of tuna (raw no less), micro greens and a handful of fried chicken skins. I still get all kinds of dirty thoughts at the mere mention of this. Or how he manages to pimp up just a simple maple glazed bacon chop to some super next level shizz. Gawd, that bacon. I'm not sure I could describe it here without relegating this book to the Adult Reference section and going all 50 shades of Mills and Boon on ya.

And then, just when U thought he couldn't top his last crazy ass creation, he goes pulls a fatality move and creates a mac & cheese but.... using.....

Get over HERE!!

wait...for...it......

BEE. TAI. MAK.

So it became, BeetaiMAK & CHEESE.

BOOM. DINGPINGDING. FLAWLESS VICTORY.

So BRACE YOURSELVES, KIDS.
STRAP YOURSELF IN,
TURN THE LIGHTS DOWN,
PUT IN SOME 80's ROCK & ROLL,
AND GET READY
FOR A DELICIOUSLY HAIRY
RIDE THROUGH THE ZANY
WORLD
OF
BJORN &
TEAM ARTICHOKE.

~~LOVE~~ DAMN you.

goz.

Goz Lee

Author of *Plusixfive: A Singaporean Supper Club Cookbook*

Notes from an Artichoke Stalker

It was a late-ish evening in June 2011, and I was looking for a non-Asian joint that didn't serve the standard 'Western' fare of cream of mushroom soup and braised beef cheeks. Then I found a spot for 'modern Moorish cuisine... inspired by the fascinating flavours and smells of Turkey, Lebanon, Greece and Morocco.' At the time in Singapore, outside of Kampong Glam, this was akin to uncovering chwee kuay in Warsaw. I was hot off an assignment in Turkey and pining for legitimate mezzes. When the Forgotten Grain Salad—a tumble of quinoa, bulgur, wild rice, capers, seeds, nuts, fruits and herbs crowned with labneh—hit the table, my heart set sail on the Bosphorous. I prayed that Artichoke would never choke.

"I'm not an overly religious man!" Bjorn once declared to me. So, in effect, he never needed my prayers. His maverick ways about the kitchen, doing unthinkable yet completely logical things to ingredients from kale to quail, were enough. I've seen fennel and Tahitian vanilla salad; sticky duck in pomegranate molasses and pistachios; and the climax of any evening—the Lambgasm, a massive boner of meat-stasy. And then there was brunch. What started innocently as ful medames and lamb shakshouka morphed into taste bud throwdowns where fried chicken was crowned with marshmallows and a sausage-and-bacon pie floated in a popcorn-and-corn puree. You won't find anything like this in Singapore or beyond, just as you'd never expect bak chor mee in Denmark. Unless you invite Bjorn to the vaunted Copenhagen Cooking food festival and he ensconces our national noodle dish within a pillowy soft bun for the occasion.

A Singaporean can lose his or her appetite futzing over who will continue our hawker legacies, or over the indigestible reality that more and more of our heritage food arrives pre-made in a factory for someone to reheat at a stall. But Bjorn is part of a new chef's revolution, creating a brand of Singaporean cooking that we should be just as proud of. With his trademark stubbornness, Bjorn has committed at least 30 per cent of Artichoke's menu to local ingredients, after hours spent haranguing small local farms to sell him their best produce. So the incredibly fresh flavours that explode in your mouth are not simply the result of Bjorn's 'dude food' wit that seasons all his creations. They are also the result of an agricultural awakening. I never knew how massive abalone mushrooms could get in Kranji.

Artichoke no longer goes by that polite 'modern Moorish cuisine' tagline, but a cheeky 'deviant Middle Eastern food.' Thank heavens, because dessert then was malabi topped with chilled sliced grapes. Yeah. These days, it's bodacious baklava and a seriously sick Snickers tart, among other things (like a custom-made Kit Kat fortress masquerading as cake). If this is what the future of food looks like here, let's chow down the New Wok Order.

Desiree Koh
Writer

Why Write This Book?

>>>>>

PART I

While choosing a name for my restaurant, I tried every possible method. I brainstormed for nights on end, thinking up words and all their possible connotations. I eventually arrived at a shortlist of eight; some of them were good, some less so.

There was Squid Inc. The Common Room. Grub. The Mole Hole. Three Black Moles (because there is a perfect equilateral triangle on my noggin that is formed by exactly that). I ran these names by my family and close friends. There was no unanimous agreement on which name sounded right; everyone had his or her own opinion. After all the hard work put in, it started to get frustrating. I realised that even amongst the people closest to me, there was no one name that would please them all.

So I said what has since become my three-word strategic business motto—fuck this shit—and went off the beaten path. I grabbed *Food: The Definitive Guide* off the shelf, flipped to a random page, closed my eyes and poked at it with my index finger. The word it landed on would be the name of my restaurant.

I opened my eyes. BEGINNING. Whaaaaaaat? Hell, no—'beginning'? Ok, try again. I shut my eyes again, flipped the pages, and hoped for fuck's sake I wouldn't get another dumb word… Boom! ARTICHOKE. Ok, that wasn't so bad. And that was that.

This pretty much sums up the story and ethos behind my restaurant. I'd always try to plan something in a tried-and-true, organised and responsible way; I'd run it by people to get their

I grabbed *Food: The Definitive Guide* off the shelf, flipped to a random page, closed my eyes and poked at it with my index finger. The word it landed on would be the name of my restaurant.

But what little we did know, we brandished wildly like cavemen's clubs, slinging out stuff we felt tasted good. That was as intricate as our game plan ever got—to make food that tasted good.

responses; they'd all give me different answers; the whole exercise would start to go nowhere; I'd eventually say "fuck this shit" and do it my way; it would all work out in the end. These days, I just skip straight to that last step.

So Artichoke was a restaurant born out of impulse and recklessness. Four years on, it's also a testament to how an enterprise started on such a fucked up approach could actually succeed. Here's what I mean.

We started out trying to be a contemporary Middle Eastern restaurant. I chose this particular cuisine because a) I wanted to try something different, b) I had a few Arab, Iranian, and Turkish mates back in Australia where I lived previously, and c) I enjoyed the food they ate at home when I went to visit. No other reasons apart from these.

We didn't want to appear too 'ethnic', so we steered away from doner kebabs and Turkish tea. No shisha, no belly dancers. Operating a Middle Eastern restaurant in Singapore without the all-expected shawarma and shisha was like signing a death sentence, but we did it anyway. We never had staff from the region; none of us had Middle Eastern grandmas or grew up eating hummus and lavash. Damn, I'd never been there myself, and here I was, throwing together a motley crew of cooks who themselves had almost no experience in Middle Eastern cooking. (Till today, customers are shocked to find out the head chef is not Middle Eastern, but a Singaporean dude with a **pervert moustache**.) But what little we did know, we brandished wildly like cavemen's clubs, slinging out stuff we felt tasted good. That was as intricate as our game plan ever got—to make food that tasted good.

Everything we rolled out from the kitchen, we were doing for the absolute first time. And we served it to members of the paying public whose evaluations had the power to make or break us. Everything about it was wrong. **IT SHOULD NOT HAVE WORKED.**

But somehow it did. Yeah, the food was (and is) good, but somehow, **we also ended up in the right place at the right time, with the right people supporting us**. And I don't know how much longer this wave of dumb luck will last.

So, Artichoke isn't just a book of gnarly recipes that have made an appearance at the restaurant at some time or other. It's also a documentation of utterly unforeseen success, complete with foul language, cuts, scrapes, burns, tattoos, bad customers, great customers, brunch slams, street punks, and bacon. Lots of bacon. (See Chapter 13: Bacon is Evil, We Must Destroy it with Our Teeth.)

It's a chance to relish every last inch of this crazy journey while I can, and I'd like to invite you to come along with me and rock out with your fork out.

PART II

How To Use This Book Or, How To

★ ROCK OUT WITH ★ YOUR FORK OUT

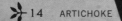

》》》》》

There are many great cookbooks out there that lay out, in exacting detail, how to poach an egg, butterfly a prawn or set up charcoal for a barbecue. This book isn't one of them. What you hold in your hands isn't meant to teach you how to cook; it is more a way for me to share my ideas with you.

Essentially, it's an ideas book, not a this-is-how-you-do-it one. I'd like you to be inspired by what you read and then go off and riff on it, just as I myself have never replicated someone else's recipe gram for gram, minute for minute. When you look at the pictures in here, I want you to have mental orgasms. I'd be ecstatic if you consider the recipes more as basic guidelines for your personal interpretation of the dishes.

Our taste buds differ, from person to person—what is salty to you may not be salty to me; you may have a high tolerance for spiciness while I don't. Ingredients are different too—wherever in the world you are right now, produce and the degree of their flavours will vary. Lemons from your market could be much less acidic than the ones I use in my restaurant; different brands of yoghurt have different fat content and hence different textures. My recipes are written bearing in mind the ingredients that are available in my neck of the woods, as well as my personal threshold for salt, sugar, acidity, spiciness, etc.

But don't freak out—just trust yourself and do it your way. Feel free to use more of this and less of that; listen to your gut. Don't feel obliged to follow the recipes word for word. The important thing is to taste constantly as you cook. Obviously, don't be an idiot and lick raw pork—you know what I mean. Remember, you're not cooking for me; you're cooking for yourself. All that matters is that it tastes good to you.

So, with this in mind, let loose. The goal of this book is to rid you (somewhat) of common sense and to get you cooking dangerously, with ingredient combinations that you'd have never thought of otherwise. If you like the idea of donuts topped with chicken skin crackling, go make some. If you've long wondered what would happen if you deep-fried a whole head of cabbage, then get off your ass and find out.

The goal of this book is to rid you (somewhat) of common sense and to get you cooking dangerously.

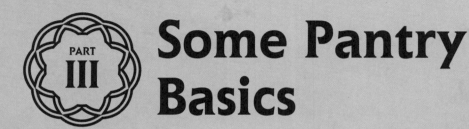

PART III

Some Pantry Basics

>>>>>

I'm well aware that there may be a few ingredients and methods among these recipes that could be unfamiliar. To smoothen things out, here are a couple of pointers to get you started.

HALOUMI

Haloumi is a Mediterranean cheese, originally from Cyprus, that's made from a mixture of goat's and sheep's milk. It's great for grilling and pan-frying because it holds its shape well when cooked, becoming squeaky and squishy instead. Kinda like bubble gum. You can find haloumi in the cheese sections of supermarkets such as Jasons The Gourmet Grocer and Cold Storage.

All the haloumi imported into Singapore is vacuum-packed. If you cook it straight from the pack, it'll suck. It will be dry, powdery, and extremely salty, without the characteristic squishiness. What you need to do is bring it back to life first. How? Easy.

Remove the cheese from its package and soak it completely submerged in cold water for 6 or more hours. Change the water every 2 hours or so. This process purges the haloumi of excess salt, and helps rehydrate the insides. Now you'll have 'fresh' haloumi again. To cook, pat the block dry with some kitchen paper, slice it into 1 to 2cm-thick slices, and pan-fry over medium heat for 1 to 2 minutes on each side.

You'll notice the recipes call for a 'block' of haloumi, which refers to standard package sizes ranging from 180 to 250g.

BULGUR

Bulgur is a dry high-fibre, high-protein cereal made from cracked wheat grains which have been earlier steamed and dried. This makes it 'cook' very fast because, technically, it is already cooked. In Singapore, there are two kinds of bulgur available: fine and coarse. We use fine bulgur for dishes like tabbouleh where all we're after is a light fluffy texture (page 39), similar to couscous. Coarse bulgur is used for heavier dishes like a bulgur pilaf. You can find the grain in the health foods section of Cold Storage, or in health food stores such as Brown Rice Paradise in Tanglin Mall.

Preparing bulgur is very easy. If using the fine version, soak the grains in tap water for 5 to 7 minutes and drain off the excess water. Spread out onto a flat tray to dry for 10 to 20 minutes. The grains should be soft enough to chew through, but have a firm inner core, much like al dente pasta or risotto. Fluff it up with a fork and toss it through your salads.

For coarse bulgur, the process is similar, but you'll have to soak the grains anywhere from 45 minutes to an hour.

SUMAC

Sumac is a dried, ground fruit that has a zesty, lemony flavour. It is widely used in Middle Eastern cuisine to add a burst of brightness to salads, mezzes and grilled meats. Since it is a dry condiment that gives a lemony flavour, we've used it to flavour crispy things whose crusts we don't want to soggify. For example, instead of squeezing a wedge of lemon over a piece of crispy beer-battered fish, why not sprinkle some sumac instead? We've taken this same approach with our dish of Fish Fries (page 99). You can find sumac at gourmet grocers such as Culina and Jones the Grocer.

ORANGE BLOSSOM WATER AND ROSEWATER

These are two staples in the Middle Eastern pantry. They are basically distillations of orange blossoms and rose petals, respectively. They add a lovely perfume to any dish, but you'll have to be very careful about how you use them because too much in a dish can be overpowering and make you think that you just licked Grandma's perfume spritzer. A few drops really go a long way. You can find rosewater in most Indian provision shops or in the infallible Mustafa Centre. Orange blossom water can be found at gourmet grocers or at our bakery, Overdoughs.

FLATBREAD

Let's face it, we don't live in a country where Arabian-style flatbread can be picked up at the neighbourhood bakery. In fact, flatbreads are so hard to find in Singapore that many doner kebab places resort to using flour tortillas (the kind used for burritos) to wrap their kebabs. However, if you look hard enough, you'll find some specialty supermarkets periodically stocking flatbreads like pitas and naan (not Middle Eastern, but close enough). You can use any of these when a recipe here calls for flatbread, but do remember that these are pre-packaged, highly processed breads. You'll need to follow the package's instructions on how to reheat lest you end up with something really nasty. Alternatively, just go to a North Indian joint and take home a couple of slices of freshly made naan. That's my best advice.

FRESH HERBS

Nothing beats the flavour of fresh herbs when finishing off a dish. My advice on using herbs is to throw them into the dish at the very last possible moment, so that they keep their vibrancy. It's hard to measure fresh herbs in terms of weight, because they are so light; it's also hard to measure them in terms of spoons or cups because they tend not to fit into these vessels. The best way I can describe how much herbs to use in a dish is by handfuls. It's quite easy to do: using the tips of all five fingers, loosely pick up as much herbs as you can without squashing them. Don't be greedy and try to grab with your entire palm: you'll just bruise them.

TOASTING NUTS AND SEEDS

Many of the recipes here in this book call for nuts and seeds—such as cumin seeds, coriander seeds, pistachios, almonds etc.—to be toasted. I find that the resulting warm, robust flavour can take a dish to the next level. Some people toast them in a pan over low heat while others do so over high heat. Some others use the oven. Here's my favourite style.

Grab a heavy-based frying pan or a cast-iron pan and heat it up, dry, till it's smoking. Throw in your nuts or seeds, turn the heat off and keep tossing the seeds in the pan. Because the pan is so thick that it holds its heat, the nuts and seeds should toast very evenly in a short time if you stir them constantly. Once they darken and begin to release a fragrant aroma after 1 to 2 minutes, transfer to a plate to cool.

This technique will not work with thin, cheap non-stick pans. Those don't hold heat well, and will cool down as soon as you take them off the heat.

DEEP-FRYING STUFF

As you may have already noticed, many of the recipes in this book involve deep-frying. (That's just how I roll.) While owning a deep fryer would make things a hell lot easier for you, it's no problem if you don't. One way of ensuring the oil is up to the required temp is to use a deep-fry thermometer. If that isn't readily available, simply take a wooden utensil—say, bamboo chopstick or slotted wooden spatula—and dip it into the hot oil. If the oil immediately starts to sizzle and bubble around the implement, it's ready for deep-frying. Try not to crowd the pot with too much food as this will lower the temperature of the oil. It's better to cook in several small batches than to dump a whole load into the mix.

When deep-frying meat, it might be prudent to single out one sacrificial piece. When you think the meat's about done, fish out a piece and slice into it to see if it's cooked through. If it's still bloody on the inside, leave the rest to cook a little longer.

All the recipes specify vegetable oil, which has a high smoke point. Other suitable varieties are peanut, canola and grape seed oils.

CHAPTER 1

The Little Place with No Signboard

>>>>>>

May 2010. I was wiped out. I had spent the past few months jobless and looking for a space to open my very first restaurant. Months had gone by without any luck; I almost threw in the towel on the project several times and was starting to seriously consider accepting a head chef job offer at a boutique hotel in Chinatown.

Then came along this gorgeous little space at 161 Middle Road. As it is with these things, the father of a friend knew someone who knew someone who managed the property. I knew the place—then, a café called My Secret Garden occupied the premises. In fact, I'd been there on several dates in previous years (none of which worked out, by the way). Before places like Rochester Park and Dempsey Hill—with their colonial black and white houses—were converted into dining enclaves, My Secret Garden was probably one of the first restaurant spots in the CBD built like a home, with its private cobblestone courtyard, sunroom and all. It was such a welcome oasis in the middle of town. Each time I visited, I'd always thought how killer it would be to have a place like that one day.

I suddenly found myself talking to management. Apparently, My Secret Garden was vacating in a month. I told them about my idea for Artichoke. A month later, they handed me the keys.

I opened with close to nothing. There were no big investors to back me up. I was in this on my own—it was make it or break it. I took a small loan from my granddad and just went in balls first. The starting budget was laughable, and I could barely afford many

I'd always thought how killer it would be to have a place like that one day.

Pots, pans and $1 plates were bargained for at run down repo shops in secluded industrial estates. Fancy was frivolous.

things. I bought second-hand kitchen equipment with dodgy one-month warranties. I crammed my grandma's little Honda Jazz with furniture as I shuttled back and forth between my restaurant-to-be and the Salvation Army thrift store. Pots, pans and $1 plates were bargained for at run down repo shops in secluded industrial estates. Fancy was frivolous; I just needed enough to get the restaurant up and running.

And that was the case with pretty much everything else. My uncle Daniel gave me mates' rates on the renovation, promising to rip me off on my next project if I were successful on this one. While discussing the budget, he asked me how much money I could set aside for wall fittings and design—things like shelves, panelling, interior artwork and such.

"Nada," I said, "Just paint everything black and I'll write on it like a chalkboard."

Next, he asked me about signage.

"Fuck it, I'll write that in chalk too."

So here we were, August 2010. Artichoke opened with zero pre-launch hype or marketing. A small restaurant opened by a nobody, with no proper signage, no frills and no turning back.

For a while that kinda sucked. Besides my family and friends, no one knew we existed. The only other people who came were old patrons looking for My Secret Garden. Ronny, my restaurant manager, would smoke a cigarette in Waterloo Street and hustle passers-by like a hardworking strip club promoter. When they came in and saw our menu, most turned and walked away.

After a month of this, we were getting nervous. Antsy. Why was no one coming? We were, I figured, being too cheffy. Trying to introduce an updated, sexy take on Middle Eastern cuisine, with dishes like pearl barley tabbouleh and lamb ribs with date molasses was, perhaps, too far ahead of the curve at the time. What was worse, we had no existing brand credibility.

We put our egos aside and took the menu down a coupla notches. Ambitious, overly fancy shit just wouldn't cut it right now. Dishes had to be approachable and familiar enough to a local market and palate.

So we hooked our dishes back to recognizable reference points—training wheels for Middle Eastern fare, if you will.

People like French toast; they got baklava French toast with pistachios and rose yoghurt. Everyone knows what meatballs are; we served them in spiced tomato sauce and labneh. Boston clam chowder was Arabicized as a fish and mussel chowder with a drizzle of za'atar oil.

We had somehow cornered ourselves into a strange hybrid of Middle Eastern-inspired food and mainstream café fare. I wasn't entirely happy with the new direction, but time was ticking, money was walking, and we needed to get butts on seats, pronto.

Time was ticking, money was walking, and we needed to get butts on seats, pronto.

" I was in this on my own—it was make it or break it. **"**

SERVES 4

MEATBALLS
Vegetable oil, for frying
½ medium white onion,
    finely chopped
1 tsp fennel powder
2 tsp cumin powder
2 tsp black pepper
400 g minced beef
1 egg, beaten
4 cloves garlic, finely chopped
1 tbsp breadcrumbs
1 tbsp milk
Pinch of salt

SPICED TOMATO SAUCE
½ cup olive oil
2 tsp cumin powder
2 tsp fennel powder
2 tsp smoked paprika
1 tsp black pepper
1 cinnamon stick
1 medium white onion,
    finely chopped
3 cloves garlic, finely chopped
4 cups finely chopped tomatoes
1 bay leaf
1 tsp honey
Salt and pepper

3 tbsp salted butter
1 cup breadcrumbs
4 tbsp vegetable oil
½ cup labneh (page 260)
1 handful fresh herbs (such as
    parsley, coriander and mint)
Extra virgin olive oil, for drizzling

MEATBALLS
IN SPICED TOMATO SAUCE AND LABNEH

Meatballs have this ability to transcend cultural boundaries. This was one of the dishes that we put on our menu in the early days to give new customers a familiar and comforting reference point. Labneh, a thick yoghurt cheese, rounds out the acidity of the tomato sauce and adds a lovely richness to the dish.

»»»»

To make the meatballs, heat the vegetable oil over medium heat in a frying pan. Add the onions and sauté till translucent and sweet. Add the fennel, cumin and pepper, and toast for about a minute, till fragrant. Let cool. Combine this onion-spice mix lightly with the rest of the meatball ingredients. Season with salt. Cook a small portion in a frying pan for a taste test. Add more salt if necessary. Shape into golf ball-sized balls and refrigerate to firm them up slightly.

To make the sauce, heat up the olive oil over medium heat in a heavy-based saucepan and cook the spices, onion and garlic for 2 to 3 minutes till the onions are soft. Add the tomatoes, bay leaf and honey. Bring to a simmer for 20 to 30 minutes, until the tomatoes start to break down and the onions get really sweet. Season to taste with salt and pepper.

Heat the butter in a frying pan over medium heat. Add the bread-crumbs and toast until they turn crisp. Drain on kitchen paper. Heat the vegetable oil in a frying pan over medium-high heat, and sear the meatballs on all sides for 3 minutes, or until golden-brown. Add the meatballs to the sauce and simmer for 6 to 8 minutes, until they are cooked 80 per cent through. Serve on a platter with dollops of labneh, a scattering of breadcrumbs, some fresh herbs and a generous splash of extra virgin olive oil.

FISH AND MUSSEL CHOWDER
WITH TURKISH CROUTONS AND ZA'ATAR OIL

SOUP

2 tbsp olive oil

3 tbsp unsalted butter

4 medium shallots, chopped

4 cloves garlic, chopped

½ cup chopped carrot

½ cup chopped celery

3 tbsp plain flour

1 sprig thyme

2 cups fish stock (feel free
   to use a good quality
   store-bought stock)

½ cup white wine

3 cups milk

1 cup heavy cream

1 large russet potato, chopped

Salt and pepper

400 g mussels, scrubbed

CROUTONS

2 tbsp olive oil

1 handful torn or
   cubed Turkish bread

Sea salt

Pinch of za'atar

2 tbsp unsalted butter

1 tbsp olive oil

400 g white fish fillets (such as
   snapper, cod or sea bass)

Salt and pepper

2 tbsp za'atar

4 tbsp extra virgin olive oil

1 tbsp chopped chives

A few pieces oil-packed semi-
   or sun-dried tomatoes (optional)

Another one of the dishes we served in our first months of trade to get butts on seats. We hoped the unthreatening idea of a chowder—as seen at joints like Mos Burger and Fish & Co.—would act as 'training wheels' in our effort to expose locals to za'atar, an intoxicatingly fragrant mixture of dried wild thyme and other herbs, sumac and sesame seeds. You'll be able to find za'atar at gourmet grocers in Singapore.

»»»»

To make the soup, heat the olive oil and butter in a heavy-based stockpot over medium heat. Add in the shallots, garlic, carrot and celery and sweat them for 4 to 5 minutes, until translucent and sweet. Add the flour and stir constantly to form a roux. Add the thyme, fish stock and wine, bring to a boil and whisk out all visible lumps. Once smooth, add the milk, cream and potatoes and simmer for 20 minutes. Season well with salt and pepper. Add the mussels and cook for 3 to 4 minutes, just until the shells open up. Discard any mussels whose shells refuse to open. Turn off the heat and keep warm.

While the soup is cooking, prepare the croutons. In a frying pan, heat up the olive oil over medium heat and add the bread. Toast till the croutons are golden and crispy throughout. Season to taste with sea salt and a pinch of za'atar, then drain on kitchen paper. Set aside.

Heat up the butter and olive oil over medium-high heat in a non-stick frying pan. Add the fish fillets and cook for 2 to 3 minutes on each side, until the fillets are cooked through. Season the fillets well with salt and pepper. Divide the soup across four serving bowl and top each with a piece of fish and a scattering of croutons. Mix the za'atar with the extra virgin olive oil and drizzle some of the mixture over each bowl. Finish each bowl with a sprinkle of chives and a few pieces of dried tomatoes.

RAS EL HANOUT

1 tsp coriander seeds

1 tsp cumin seeds

1 tsp fennel seeds

6 green cardamom pods,
    seeds only, husks discarded

2 tsp sweet or mild paprika powder

1 tsp allspice powder

1 tsp turmeric powder

1 tsp cayenne pepper

10 cloves garlic, peeled

½ cup olive oil

1 tbsp unsalted butter

8 medium-sized prawns, butterflied

1 medium lime, cut into 8 wedges

Sea salt

A small handful of
    coriander leaves, torn

Crusty bread (such as baguettes,
    ciabatta, etc.), to serve

GARLICKY PRAWNS
WITH RAS EL HANOUT AND LIME

This is our own little twist on the Spanish gambas al ajillo (garlic shrimp), while introducing the flavours of ras el hanout, an aromatic Moroccan spice blend. Ras el hanout literally means 'top of the shop', and each spice vendor has his own special blend. Here's ours.

»»»»

To make the ras el hanout, mix all the spices and toast until fragrant (page 19). Grind finely in a spice mill or a pestle and mortar.

Smash the cloves of garlic with the bottom of a saucepan (or any hard implement). Heat the oil and butter in a frying pan or heavy cast-iron pan over medium heat. Add the garlic and let it sizzle away for a minute, stirring constantly to ensure it doesn't burn. Swirl in 1 tablespoon of ras el hanout and immediately place the prawns and lime wedges into the pan. Sauté for 3 to 4 minutes over high heat till the prawns are cooked through. Season to taste with sea salt and scatter the coriander leaves over. Serve piping hot with warm, crusty bread to mop up all that spicy, garlicky, oily goodness.

POACHED APRICOTS

½ cup dried apricots, halved
1 stick cinnamon
2 star anises
1 green cardamom pod,
    seeds only, husks discarded
4 tbsp clear honey
½ cup white sugar
1 cup water

BAKLAVA FRENCH TOAST

8 eggs
1 cup heavy cream
1 tsp cinnamon powder
4 tbsp clear honey
Zest of ½ a lemon
1 tsp orange blossom water
    (optional, page 17)
4 thick slices of bread (brioche,
    ciabatta, Pullman bread, etc.)
4 tbsp unsalted butter

ROSE YOGHURT

1 cup Greek yoghurt
2 tsp rosewater
1 pinch dried rose petals (optional)

1 handful pistachios, toasted and
    coarsely chopped (page 19)

BAKLAVA FRENCH TOAST

WITH POACHED APRICOTS, PISTACHIOS AND ROSE YOGHURT

**Baklava was another easy entry point into 'Middle Easterning'
a brunch dish. We paired the elements associated with baklava
—nuts, honey, rosewater, dried apricots—with the ubiquity of
French toast, something everyone could relate to.**

»»»»

Make the poached apricots one day ahead. Place all the ingredients
in a saucepan and bring to a simmer. Allow to simmer for 15
minutes, then turn off the heat and leave to cool. Transfer to the
fridge to chill overnight.

To make the French toast, beat the eggs in a large bowl with the
cream, cinnamon powder, honey, lemon zest and orange blossom
water. Lay out the bread slices in a baking tray with high sides, and
pour the egg batter over. Allow the bread to sit in the batter for 4 to
6 minutes, to really soak it up to the core. You can ensure maximum
soaking by flipping the bread every minute or two. Heat the butter
in a frying pan over low heat and fry the bread slices for about 3
minutes on each side.

To make the rose yoghurt, mix the Greek yoghurt with the rosewater
and the dried rose petals.

To serve, lay a slice of French toast on each of four individual plates.
Divide the poached apricots across the plates. Dollop some rose
yoghurt over the apricots and sprinkle liberally with the pistachios.
Drizzle with leftover syrup from the poached apricots.

EAT
WITH ABANDON

SERVES
4

4 pieces flatbread (page 18)

Extra virgin olive oil, for drizzling

4 large eggs

Vegetable oil, for frying

4 tbsp hummus
  ('Cheaterbug' Hummus, page 254,
  or store-bought hummus)

A few thin slices of red onion,
  to garnish

4 thick slices of a good,
  crunchy tomato

Sea salt

Dukka, to garnish (page 252)

½ handful fresh mint
  or basil, shredded

OPEN SANDWICH OF

HUMMUS, DUKKA AND FRIED EGG

We wanted a clean, fresh dish on the brunch menu—and this flavourful vegetarian option was a winner. The combination of dukka and fried egg is one I cannot stress enough, and one that is completely undersold everywhere else. The contrast of nutty, crumbly dukka with the rich smoothness of a fried egg is phenomenal. I honestly don't know of any other chef who exalts this pairing as much as I do.

»»»»»

To warm up the flatbread, spray each piece with a little water and warm over medium heat in a pan for 1 minute on each side. Drizzle immediately with extra virgin olive oil.

While the bread is warming up, fry the four eggs sunny-side up. Heat up the vegetable oil over high heat in a non-stick frying pan. Crack in one egg and cook to the point where the whites get crispy around the edges but the yolks are still runny. Remove and repeat with the other three eggs, adding more oil as necessary.

Spread each slice of toasted bread with a heaped tablespoon of hummus, then top with the onions and a slice of tomato. Sprinkle sea salt on the tomato to really make its flavour pop. Slide a sunny-side up egg over each tomato and scatter a pinch of dukka over each yolk. Sprinkle the top of each egg with the herbs and add a final drizzle of extra virgin olive oil.

The contrast of nutty, crumbly dukka with the rich smoothness of a fried egg is phenomenal.

CHAPTER 2

No Doner Kebabs, No Persian Carpets

Potential customer: What kind of food do you serve?

Us: Hi there, we serve modern Middle Eastern food!

Potential customer: *(Studies the menu for a minute)* Why don't you have kebabs?

Us: Oh, good question. We don't consider ourselves traditional, and we offer something a little different from what you get at other Middle Eastern restaurants. We have really good meat dishes though, like our 7-spice meatballs with labneh, and our garlic prawns with ras el hanout. Wanna grab a seat and try us out?

Potential customer: *(Obviously not listening to a word we're saying)* So you don't have falafel?

Us: No, sorry. Not at the moment.

Potential customer: Let me guess—no Turkish coffee.

Us: Nope, but we do have other nice drinks. Here, have a look at our drink lis….

Potential customer: What kind of a Middle Eastern restaurant are you?

Us: Well, we're…

Potential customer-no-more: Forget it. *(Walks away)*

This; this was the soundtrack of our first 6 months. People calling us out on every Middle Eastern food cliché we didn't have. Doner kebabs, falafel, rice pilaf, Persian carpets, shisha, Arabic music, belly

dancers. On the other end of the spectrum, we had people mouthing off at us for not having steak, pasta, pizza, balsamic vinegar, ketchup or smoothies. On more than one occasion, customers would look at our menu and ask: **"Where's your real food?"**

At first, my crew and I were stymied. As it sank in, we were slightly bemused. When it really sank in, we were deeply perturbed. Trying to balance what we wanted to be with what people expected us to be was truly mind-bending. Finally, we said, "SCREW IT."

As Eddie Huang, the very inspiring original gangsta of NYC's BaoHaus, said at the Big Omaha 2012 conference: "If people don't get it, I don't care. I just do what I do; they can catch up… If I make a big enough impact, Wikipedia will explain that shit to them."

I listened to those wise words of validation with awe in my gaze and wood in my pants. I'd only found the video on YouTube two years after Artichoke had gone through its trying phase. Bruised and battered, we had unwittingly stumbled upon the Eddie Huang Culinary Nirvana on our own, where we stopped giving a fuck about ticking people's boxes. I was a man on the edge, and I was prepared to lose it all. If Artichoke crashed and burned because of this decision, then at least we went down on our own bloody terms.

From that day on, we stopped trying to figure people out and started cooking whatever the hell we wanted to. We returned to base zero. No more pandering to demands for kid's menus, truffle fries and eggs Benedict. No more 'Middle Eastern' chickpea-battered fish and chips or Middle Eastern-inspired meatballs. They were good, but woefully transparent. Unexciting. Instead, we were bringing sexy back with full-on creative shit, just like how we meant to at the beginning: contemporary, sexy, progressive versions of Middle Eastern food. There were kisirs, tabboulehs, yoghurt soups. Merguez, shakshouka and harira. But we took them one step further by injecting an artisanal approach. Quinoa and raw corn kernels made an appearance in tabbouleh. Our version of chilled yoghurt soup—traditionally a watered-down cucumber tzatziki—infused yoghurt with a ton of fresh market veggies. Never mind that some customers had problems pronouncing the names of dishes—it was high time the crew stormed the cockpit, regained the controls, and steered the plane back on its intended path.

I was a man on the edge, and I was prepared to lose it all.

Guess what? Our gamble worked. We realised we'd been too impatient before, with too little conviction in our brand. People started trickling in, swelling to a steady flow by the end of six months. A couple of good reviews in the press helped tremendously. People actually liked us! With a solidly deepening customer base, we could afford to take chances—reckless chances—with our food. The menu took on a slightly schizophrenic vibe. Four years on, we still have 'serious', pimped up interpretations of Middle Eastern dishes, like **Lebanese smoked chicken** with toum (page 64) and slow-roasted lamb shoulder. But on the other end of the spectrum, we can now indulge our sickest fantasies and foist deviant, so-bad-it's-good wonders upon our willing guests: falafel-battered fish nuggets with potato chip tabbouleh, for one, or bacon hotdog pie floaters with Tiger Beer cheese soup. I mean, with a crazy mofo—yours truly—at the helm, it was bound to happen sooner or later. That's one of the perks of owning your own restaurant, clichés be damned.

We are not a "western" restaurant. Please do not ask us why we do not serve eggs benedict, waffles, ketchup, tobasco, pizza & hamburgers Thank u Stay awesome

DRESSING

1 tbsp lemon juice
½ clove garlic, finely chopped
½ tsp allspice
½ tsp cinnamon powder
1 tsp sumac (page 17)
½ cup extra virgin olive oil
Salt and pepper

120 g rocket, washed, dried
   and coarsely chopped
1 corn ear's worth of fresh, raw kernels
2 large tomatoes,
   de-seeded, drained of
   excess juices, finely chopped
¼ red onion, finely chopped
1 stalk spring onion, finely chopped
1 handful fresh mint, finely chopped
½ cup fine bulgur or coarse bulgur,
   soaked and air-dried (page 17)
Salt and pepper

ROCKET AND SWEET CORN
TABBOULEH

'Tabbouleh' was another exotic word we threw in there to pique people's interest. The dish hails from the Levantine region, which today spans Israel, Jordan, Lebanon, Syria, Palestine, Turkey and the islands of Cyprus. To tweak the dish for a local palate, we replaced parsley—always a polarizing herb—with the less assertive rocket. We also used raw corn for its surprising pops of sweetness and texture, and to show off how wonderful the raw vegetable can taste.

》》》》》

To make the dressing, place all the ingredients into a mixing bowl and whisk till well combined. Season to taste with salt and pepper.

Combine the rocket and the rest of the vegetables in a large bowl. Add in the bulgur and fluff everything up with your hands, then pour in the dressing bit by bit until the vegetables are just coated. You may or may not use up all the dressing. Mix well, and season to taste further with salt and pepper. Serve this salad in a communal salad dish for guests to pass round the table.

> **"** We stopped trying to figure people out and started cooking whatever the hell we wanted to. **"**

1 handful fresh coriander

1 handful fresh dill

2 cloves garlic, peeled

Zest of 1 lemon, finely grated

1 green capsicum, cored and
finely chopped

3 sticks celery, finely chopped

2 large Japanese cucumbers,
peeled and finely chopped

2 large tomatoes, finely chopped

350 g Greek yogurt

200 ml cold vegetable stock
or plain water

150 ml extra virgin olive oil,
plus additional for drizzling

1 tbsp lemon juice

Salt and pepper

Fresh, finely chopped herbs
(basil, dill, mint, and chives)
and flowers*, to garnish

*You can find packs of
colourful, ready-to-eat edible
flowers at gourmet grocers.

HADI'S COLD YOGHURT SOUP
WITH FRESH HERBS AND FLOWERS

When I was living in Brisbane as a student, I had a Persian housemate named Hadi. He'd always cook and feed me tons of stuff, half of which I'd hate and half of which I'd love. One of the dishes that grew on me was a chilled Persian yoghurt soup, typically made by whisking Greek yoghurt with ice water, cucumber and assorted herbs. At Artichoke, I decided to tweak the recipe by using a gazpacho-style approach—blending tons of fresh veggies like celery, capsicum and tomatoes with yoghurt, then brightening it up with extra virgin olive oil and some pretty flowers from our herb patch. This is an elegant dish (not a word you'll hear much more of in the rest of the book).

》》》》》

Place all the ingredients, except for the lemon juice and garnishing herbs, into a blender and blend till very smooth. You may need to do this in two or more batches, depending on the size of your blender. Season to taste with the lemon juice, salt and pepper. Chill overnight, or for at least 6 hours. Strain the soup through a fine sieve and discard the solids. If you like your soup to have more texture, withhold a quarter of the strained solids and mix them back into your soup. To serve, divide among individual bowls and garnish with the herbs, flowers and a final drizzle of extra virgin olive oil.

1 medium green chilli, finely chopped
2 cloves garlic, finely chopped
2 small shallots, finely chopped
150 g smoked oysters, finely chopped
250 g cream cheese
1 tbsp lemon juice
½ tbsp smoked paprika
1 tbsp extra virgin olive oil
Salt and pepper
2 to 3 tbsp heavy cream (optional)

SMOKED OYSTER TARAMASALATA

Taramasalata is a thick, creamy Greek and Turkish mezze made with fish roe, olive oil, breadcrumbs and seasonings. I liked the word because it created mystery, a sense of appeal. To adapt to the lack of suitable cod roe in Singapore at the time, we substituted it with smoked oyster. Apart from adding a similar brininess to the dish, the oysters' smokiness confers yet another flavour dimension. Use as a dip for anything from pita bread to raw vegetables; or serve as a crostini for a great little snack; or toss with charred broccoli (as a substitute for anchovy sauce, page 213).

»»»»

Combine all ingredients in a mixing bowl and whisk till thick and creamy, but not stiff. Season to taste with salt and pepper. If you find the mixture too stiff, thin it with some heavy cream —use your judgment here. Allow to sit for at least an hour to allow the flavours to mingle before serving.

Apart from adding a similar brininess to the dish, the oysters' smokiness confers yet another flavour dimension.

½ cup Israeli couscous (may be
    substituted with orzo or fregola)

Water, for boiling

Salt and pepper

2 tbsp olive oil

2 shallots, finely chopped

4 cloves garlic, finely chopped

½ stick celery, chopped

250 g lamb merguez sausage, casing
    removed and sausage crumbled

1 tsp ras el hanout (page 30)

1 tsp preserved lemon, finely chopped
    or zest of ½ a lemon, finely grated

½ cup cherry tomatoes, halved

500 g mussels, scrubbed

1 cup white wine (such as
    Sauvignon Blanc or Pinot Gris)

2 to 3 tbsp smen (page 254)

1 handful fresh coriander and/or
    parsley, chopped

Salt and pepper

Crusty bread (such as Turkish bread,
    sourdough, ciabatta, etc.) to serve

MUSSELS
WITH MERGUEZ SAUSAGE,
ISRAELI COUSCOUS AND SMEN

**I've always found surf and turf dishes decadent and sexy.
To diverge from the common marriages of beef and lobster
or pork and scallops, I decided to go with lamb merguez
and mussels. Like the other dishes in this chapter, this isn't a
'traditional' Middle Eastern dish—we took the common culinary
trope of pairing a meat with a shellfish, and interpreted it
within the parameters of Artichoke's 'deviant' Middle Eastern
philosophy. To nudge the dish into coherence, we took the
Moroccan origins of merguez and ran with it, including other
typically Moroccan ingredients like preserved lemon, ras el
hanout and smen.**

>>>>>

To cook the couscous, follow the manufacturer's instructions
on the packet. Make sure to boil the couscous in heavily salted
water (it should be as salty as sea water), and for only half the time
specified on the packaging. You only want to par-cook the couscous.
Every manufacturer will stipulate a different cooking time, so just
cut the time you see in the packet by half.

Heat the olive oil over medium heat in a large, heavy-based
saucepan. Add the shallots, garlic and celery and cook for 2 minutes.
Add the merguez to the saucepan, stirring every once in a while
to keep the pieces separated. Cook for 2 minutes till the pieces are
browned and 'sealed' on all sides. Add the ras el hanout, preserved
lemon and tomatoes. Cook for 1 minute more, then throw in the
mussels, wine and smen. Use as much smen as you like—I like my
mussels buttery so I usually go the full 3 tablespoons. Place a lid
over the saucepan and cook on high heat for 2 minutes. Add in the
couscous to the saucepan and cover with the lid again. Cook for 2
minutes more, or till the mussels open; discard any mussels that do
not open. Stir in the chopped herbs and season to taste with salt and
pepper. (The mussels, merguez, preserved lemon and smen are all
salty, so keep that in mind when adding extra salt).

Serve this dish in a large communal bowl. Pass around the bread to
dunk into the delicious buttery, lemony, spicy broth.

CHAPTER
3

Getting Slammed

Brunch service, by the numbers:

Every Saturday and Sunday, at 11.29am, a line forms outside our door. Sometimes 12 people long; sometimes 30. At 11.30am sharp, we open for business. In the next 5 minutes, new people keep streaming in. By 11.40am, the restaurant is half-full. 50 people place their orders within a 10-minute window. The bar and kitchen printers go loco. The moment we yank a docket off the printer, another one pops up. Our docket holders now carry 15 tables' worth of orders. The wait for food and drinks is 30 minutes. As more orders come in, it bumps up to 45 minutes. The chefs go into overdrive. All we care about is getting the food out at breakneck speed. But standards can't slip. So for the next 3 hours, we're non-stop cooking, tasting, re-cooking, re-tasting, plating. By 2.30pm, half our menu is sold out. We like it that way, because it keeps things fresh. By 2.45pm, last orders are taken. It's another mad rush as people send in their last-minute food and dessert orders. We continue pushing. By 3pm, I add up the dockets. In just over 3 hours, we've seated 52 tables and completed 186 covers, with a small crew of 6 chefs, 7 wait staff and 1 barista.

I share the count with the guys. They grin with satisfaction. Some smartass quips from around the back: "So what, last week we did 195."

In restaurant lingo, we call this insane rush 'getting slammed'. It happens every weekend at brunch. We thrive on it because it reassures us that you appreciate what we do. What makes our day even better is seeing you smile on your way out. Thank you for coming (and queuing).

For the next 3 hours, we're non-stop cooking, tasting, re-cooking, re-tasting, plating.

SPICED TOMATO SAUCE BASE

4 tbsp olive oil

3 tsp sweet paprika

1 tsp ground cumin

1 tsp ground coriander

1 medium onion, finely chopped

1 large green chilli, finely chopped

1 green capsicum, finely chopped

Salt and pepper

3 cloves garlic, finely chopped

800 g canned tomatoes, chopped

2 to 3 grabfuls of whatever you wanna
put in (anything from roast lamb to
sausages to grilled vegetables; it's
totally up to you. Just make sure
whatever you add in is already
cooked and chopped into 2 to 3cm
cubes so that it warms quickly)

4 to 6 eggs

1 handful fresh coriander,
coarsely chopped

Slices of toast, to serve

Zhoug, to serve (page 262)

SHAKSHOUKA
WITH WHATEVER YOU WANNA PUT IN

The idea of shakshouka is very simple: eggs simmered in a herb-spiked tomato sauce and eaten with bread. To bulk up the dish at Artichoke, we've created versions featuring braised lamb shank, veal meatballs, merguez sausage, roasted veggies and cheesy pumpkin. One of the most popular shakshouka fillers is lamb shoulder (page 119). We basically pluck meat off the Lambgasm, hack it up till it resembles pulled pork, heap it into the shakshouka and simmer away. I personally prefer using meatballs (page 27), as their rough-hewn texture contrasts well with the smooth sauce. A great vegetarian option is shakshouka with roasted vegetables and haloumi (page 16). Basically, this dish is a vehicle for any creativity—or mood—you wanna express.

»»»»

In a heavy-based saucepan, heat the olive oil over medium heat. Add in the paprika, cumin and coriander, and toast for 1 minute. Add in the onion, green chilli and capsicum. Season with a pinch of salt and pepper, and sweat for 7 to 10 minutes, till the vegetables turn translucent. Stir in the garlic, followed by the tomatoes a minute later. Simmer for about 10 minutes, or until the vegetables are fairly soft. Season to taste with more salt and pepper. There will be more than enough sauce for one large, communal shakshouka. You can save any leftover sauce to make another dish (e.g Meatballs in Spiced Tomato Sauce and Labneh, page 27), or another shakshouka.

To complete the dish, heat up a large frying pan or heavy cast-iron pan. Add in 2 cups of the sauce and bring to a simmer. Add in 'whatever you wanna put in' at this stage. Make small wells in the sauce and crack each egg into each well. Keeping the heat on low, cover with a lid and simmer for 3 minutes, or until the egg whites firm up but the yolks are still runny. Remove from heat while eggs are still slightly wobbly—you can tell how wobbly the eggs are simply by shaking the pan. Scatter with coriander and serve the pan in the centre of the table with slices of toast for people to dunk. Have some zhoug standing by just in case there are any spiceheads at the table looking for a chilli hit.

EAT HAPPILY

AVOCADO HUMMUS

2 large, ripe avocadoes
1 clove garlic, finely chopped
1 tbsp tahini
1 tbsp lemon juice
¼ cup extra virgin olive oil
Sea salt

SAUTÉED MUSHROOMS

4 handfuls assorted mushrooms
2 tbsp unsalted butter
Olive oil, for sautéing
1 clove garlic, finely chopped
1 sprig thyme
Salt and pepper

Olive oil, for toasting bread
   and pan-frying haloumi
4 thick slices crusty bread (Turkish
   bread, sourdough or ciabatta)
1 block haloumi, soaked and sliced
   into 2cm-thick pieces (page 16)
2 handfuls rocket
Extra virgin olive oil, for drizzling

PAN-FRIED HALOUMI
ON TOAST WITH MUSHROOMS, AVOCADO HUMMUS AND ROCKET

This dish hails from my student days in Brisbane, when I used to cook for friends and myself all the time. The simple combination of really great, earthy mushrooms, creamy avocado and the squeaky saltiness of haloumi was a failsafe brunch hit, as it proved to be at Artichoke. My recipe calls for assorted mushrooms, so feel free to pick your preferences. Refer to the Mushrooms Fried In Smen recipe (page 143) for great mushroom varieties you can use. Try not to use white button mushrooms. They're boring.

»»»»

To make the avocado hummus, peel and de-seed the avocados. Place the avocado flesh in a mixing bowl with the garlic, tahini and lemon juice. Using the prongs of a fork, crush the avocado, adding in the olive oil bit by bit to create a soft creamy texture. Season generously with sea salt and keep chilled.

Tear the mushrooms into bite-sized pieces. Heat up a large non-stick frying pan over medium-high heat. Add in the butter and a good splash of olive oil. When the butter is foamy, add in the garlic, followed immediately by the mushrooms and thyme. Season well with salt and pepper. Sauté over high heat for 2 to 3 minutes, until the mushrooms are juicy and cooked through. Transfer to a mixing bowl and keep warm.

Drizzle a little olive oil over the bread slices and toast them in a pan over medium heat. When crispy and slightly charred on the edges, set aside. Heat up a little more oil and pan-fry the haloumi for 1 to 2 minutes on each side over medium heat till golden-brown and soft to the touch. To assemble, spread each slice of toast with a quarter of the avocado hummus. Divide the mushrooms, haloumi slices and rocket across the toast slices. Drizzle with extra virgin olive oil.

MAKES
4
PIES

BEEF, SPINACH AND CHEESE BRIK

I'm always on a quest to 'dude' dishes up. Brik, a Tunisian meat pie made with crispy malsouqa pastry, finds its cross-continental counterpart in the English gravy pie. Instead of serving it deep-fried and dry, we present our brik doused in thick, fragrant beef gravy.

⟫⟫⟫

To make the beef filling, heat the oil over medium-high heat in a casserole. When the oil begins to smoke, add the beef cubes, and brown on all sides for about 5 minutes. Make sure not to crowd the pan; brown the beef in batches if necessary. Set aside.

Preheat your oven to 180°C. In the same casserole, add the onion, carrot, celery and garlic. Throw in a pinch of salt and cook over medium heat for 5 to 7 minutes, until the vegetables are soft and sweet. Add the browned beef cubes back to the casserole, along with the remaining ingredients for the beef filling. Cover the casserole

BEEF FILLING

Vegetable oil, for browning
1 kg boneless beef short ribs
   or brisket, chopped into
   2 to 3cm cubes
1 yellow onion, finely chopped
1 carrot, finely chopped
1 stick celery, finely chopped
5 cloves garlic, finely chopped
A pinch of salt
2 large tomatoes, finely chopped
2 cups beef stock
1 cup white wine
2 star anises
1 stick cinnamon
2 bay leaves

2 tbsp vegetable oil
200 g baby spinach leaves
Salt and pepper
3 tbsp unsalted butter
3 tbsp plain flour
1 cup heavy cream
8 sheets filo pastry (store-bought),
   just thawed
1 cup clarified butter
1 cup kashkaval
   or other melty cheese
   (Gruyere, Emmenthal, Camembert,
   Brie, white cheddar, etc.), grated
Roasted eggplant relish,
   to serve (page 263)
Rocket, to garnish

All that leftover filling goes
well on toast or stuffed in
a sandwich toaster. Or use
it as an awesome filler in
shakshouka (page 48).

with a lid and place in the oven. Leave for 2 to 3 hours, until the beef is fall-apart tender.

Allow the beef to cool to room temperature in its juice. Fish out the beef cubes and set aside. Strain the rest of the casserole's contents. Discard the solids while reserving the braising liquid. Set aside.

Heat the vegetable oil over medium-high heat in a pan and cook the spinach until it wilts. Season to taste with salt. Place the spinach in a colander and squeeze out as much liquid as you can. Chill in the fridge.

In a saucepan, add the butter and allow to melt over medium heat. Once the butter is bubbling, whisk in the plain flour and continue stirring for 3 minutes to achieve a golden-brown roux. Remove 1 tablespoon of the roux and set aside, then whisk the remaining roux and the heavy cream into the beef braising liquid. Season to taste with salt. What you are after at this stage is a gloopy gravy that forms a thick coating on a spoon. It should not be too watery or else it will ruin your pastry from the inside-out. If it is too thin and watery, whisk in the tablespoon of roux you set aside earlier. All flours act differently, so you'll have to use your judge ment. Season the gravy to taste with salt and pepper, and chill in the fridge.

When ready to bake, preheat your oven to 180°C. Shred the beef cubes coarsely and mix with the spinach in a bowl. Add the chilled gravy spoon by spoon, till there's just enough to coat all the beef and spinach. Brush 2 sheets of filo pastry liberally with clarified butter, and fold them lengthwise in half. Grease the base of a shallow, wide pie mould (about 2cm deep and 11.5cm in diameter) with the clarified butter, and lay on 1 sheet of folded filo pastry, allowing the excess pastry to hang over the sides. Brush the pastry with more clarified butter and place the second sheet of folded pastry 90 degrees over the first, such that the two sheets form a 'cross'. Ease the edges of the pastry into the top corners of the pie mould and sprinkle with the cheese. Spoon in the beef and spinach filling and fold the overhanging pastry back over the top to enclose the pie. Brush the top with more clarified butter and sprinkle with a pinch of salt. Repeat with the remaining 3 pies.

Bake the pies in the oven for about 30 minutes, or till the pastry is crisp. Turn the pies out of their moulds, then serve each pie piping hot with some of the warmed-up beef gravy (if there's any left over), a dollop of roasted eggplant relish and a handful of rocket leaves.

Joanna, our college intern, with lamb shakshoukas and our mezze platter.

Pomegranate arils
Handfuls of fresh mint
Cucumber, shredded into
    ribbons with a peeler
Freshly squeezed lemon juice
Sugar syrup (1 part sugar
    dissolved in 1 part water)
Cold water
Lots of ice
A few drops of orange blossom
    water or rosewater (page 17)

ARABIC LEMONADE

In Australia, I used to hang around farmers' markets each weekend for three reasons: cheap groceries, hot dogs and the amazing lemonade. The lemonade stands had huge containers, slick with condensation, with whole, freshly squeezed lemons bobbing inside the pale yellow liquid. On a hot day, a cup of this lemonade was out of this world. Here at Artichoke, I try to recreate the experience during brunch. We pimp up the recipe with herbs from our garden, add an Artichoke touch with a drop or two of orange blossom water, and serve it to the customers waiting in line on certain really hot days.

I won't furnish you with quantities here as I'd prefer you to make it to your taste.

Grab handfuls of pomegranate arils, mint leaves and cucumber ribbons and squeeze them in your hands to crush them roughly (wear latex gloves if you're icky about hygiene, like us). Place them in a large punch bowl and top with lemon juice, sugar syrup, cold water and ice. Mix and adjust the taste to your personal preference. It should taste like a nice refreshing lemonade at this stage. Here's where we take it to the next level. Add in a few drops of orange blossom water at a time and taste between each addition. You should end up with something that is lightly floral, but doesn't taste too much like Grandma's facial cream. As a general rule of thumb, 5 to 6 drops per litre of lemonade will suffice. However, every brand and bottle of orange blossom water is different, so taste as you go. Serve this at your next dinner party—your guests will be totally stoked.

The lemonade stands had huge containers, slick with condensation, with whole, freshly squeezed lemons bobbing inside the pale yellow liquid.

Vegetable oil, for frying
Frozen French fries (I like mine thick-cut)
Sea salt
Smoked paprika
Fresh mint leaves
Spring onions, finely chopped
Lemon wedges
Toum (page 253)

If you're a hardcore foodie with duck fat lying around in your fridge, cook the fries straight in duck fat, or a mix of duck fat and oil.

TOUM FRIES

Like fried eggs and dukka, fries and toum is a pairing I can't get enough of. I used to gorge on this in the Lebanese chicken and chip shops in Sydney all the time. Mind-blowing.

What I've given you here is more a guideline than a recipe. There are no specific quantities because they don't matter as much as the combination of flavours here. Make as much or as little as you want, and season the fries as much or as little as you like. Do what makes you happy!

》》》》》

Preheat the oil in a deep fryer to 180°C. If you don't have a deep fryer, heat 10cm of vegetable oil in a deep pot or saucepan over high heat till it reaches 180°C. When the oil is hot enough, cook the fries till crisp. Remove from the oil and drain in the fryer basket, or place over kitchen paper, for a few seconds.

While the fries are still super hot, toss them in a bowl with sea salt and smoked paprika. Crush the sea salt well between your thumb and index finger before sprinkling it on. This breaks it into smaller crystals that cling better to the fries. Use as much sea salt and smoked paprika as you want. I like mine seasoned quite lightly, but you may prefer yours with more flavour. Up to you.

Sprinkle some mint leaves and spring onions on top. Serve with lemon wedges and generous amounts of toum. If you've never had fries with toum before, prepare yourself for a 'wow' moment.

FUL

2 tbsp olive oil

2 tbsp unsalted butter

2 cloves garlic, finely chopped

½ white onion, finely chopped

Salt and pepper

½ green chilli, finely chopped

1 large tomato, finely chopped

½ tbsp red pepper paste
    or tomato paste

1 tbsp cumin powder

500 g canned butter beans,
    rinsed and dried

1 handful fresh coriander,
    finely chopped

Lemon juice, to garnish

4 eggs, at room temperature

Artichoke-style Pickles,
    to garnish (page 257)

Tahini Lemon Dressing,
    for drizzling (page 230)

Melted smen, for drizzling
    (optional, page 254)

1 tbsp white sesame seeds,
    toasted (page 19)

4 thick wedges of crusty bread
    or flatbread

QUICK BUTTER BEAN FUL

You'll find ful, or ful medames, everywhere on the streets in Egypt. Fava beans are stewed overnight and served with a mix of olive oil, lemon juice, garlic and chopped parsley, making for a hearty, high-energy staple dish. Instead of serving it with a boiled egg on the side—as is traditionally done—we use soft-boiled eggs that burst and infuse the dish with rich egginess as you dig in. Delicious. Fava beans are not as readily available in Singapore as other beans, so feel free to substitute with other varieties: butter, lima, navy, cannellini, borlotti, etc.

»»»»

In a heavy-based saucepan, heat the olive oil and butter over medium heat. Add the garlic and onions and allow to sweat. Season with a pinch of salt. Add in the chilli and tomato and cook for 2 to 3 minutes more, until the vegetables begin to soften. Add the red pepper paste and cumin powder, and cook for 2 minutes more. Add in the beans and enough water such that the beans are barely submerged. Simmer for 20 minutes, stirring constantly, or until the beans begin to break down and thicken the sauce. Turn off the heat. Garnish with the coriander. Add lemon juice, salt and pepper to taste.

While the ful is cooking, half-boil the eggs. Plonk the eggs in water that's at a rolling boil and leave for 5½ minutes. Remove and plunge immediately in ice water for 3 minutes. Peel the eggs and set aside.

Divide the ful across four bowls and top each bowl with an egg, the pickles, a drizzle of tahini sauce and melted smen, and the roasted sesame seeds. Dunk a wedge of bread into each bowl and serve.

Managing Customers is Like Playing Mah-jong: A Lesson in Business

CHAPTER 4

Disclaimer: As the chef-owner of my own restaurant, I am both a businessman and a service provider. A service provider's job is to make as many people as happy as possible, within reason. On the other hand, the business owner makes strategic decisions that are essential to commercial sustainability. These are two different roles that are, sometimes, diametrically opposed. I write this chapter from the perspective of the latter.

Even if you, dear reader, are not a restaurateur or in the F&B business, it's a peek into the messy mechanics of running a restaurant. And I can tell you, it ain't easy.

In mah-jong, you always start with a random hand. But as the game goes on, you draw new tiles from the deck, throw out the ones that are not good for you, and keep those that are. With each new turn, your hand gets better.

> **But as the game goes on, you draw new tiles from the deck, throw out the ones that are not good for you, and keep those that are.**

What I do is, focus on the customers that are good for the restaurant.

Mike, the cookie monster (page 71).

Managing a new customer base is pretty similar. In the early days of operation, the customers who walk through your doors are often random. They noticed you as they walked by, heard about you somewhere, or work nearby and stopped by on their lunch break. Often, these people don't know much about you, and come loaded with their own pre-determined expectations.

Just like a hand of tiles, some are good for you, and some are not. And before anyone starts getting offended at this statement, let me paint you a picture: it's the night before Roxanne's birthday. My sister-in-law only reminded me about it when she sent a text: "So where are you and Rox gonna celebrate tomorrow?" I almost crush my phone. The shops are closing in 30 minutes. I walk past a cosmetics store and make the following caveman deduction: my wife is a woman. Cosmetics are (mainly) for women. Hence, I should get her something from that store.

I have no clue what the hell I'm after; all I know is that I need it quick. I hold the single salesgirl hostage for a disproportionate amount of time, playing 20 Questions while other ladies wait for her assistance. In the time it takes to educate this caveman on the difference between blusher and mascara, three of them walk out without making a purchase. To make things worse, the poor salesgirl is one customer shy of her daily membership card sales target. I obviously don't sign up for any membership.

To sum up: in the last half hour before the store closes, I've taken up 25 minutes of the salesgirl's time, created three opportunity losses, short-changed the company of a potential membership card sale, spent a measly $150 on some common blusher that I still feel unsure of, and I'm probably never going to step in that shop again for the rest of my life. Two days later, I call them to ask for an exchange because I find out that Rox already has the blusher in the exact same shade.

The entire transaction has drained the company of more resources than my meagre expenditure can cover.

If the CEO of that make-up company informed me I was not an ideal customer, my initial reaction would, perhaps, be defensive. But considering it from his point of view, I'll understand if he never wants to see me again. Not because he doesn't like me as a person, but because I am the prime example of someone who's simply a wrong fit for his business, period. No offence taken.

My point is simple: not all customers are suitable for you. There are those who are well aligned with your brand and engage in a loving, two-way relationship, and there are those who just don't click and pose a losing battle the moment they walk in. The people who give us shit for not serving eggs Benedict might as well complain that we don't offer handjobs either. Sorry, but we just don't do those. Period. And no amount of threats of online vengeance will have us whip up an eggs benny special or manual pleasure at a moment's notice. They're better off heading to the score of other places that specialise in these things than harass us here.

Allow me to clarify: there is a stark difference between constructive and useless criticism. If someone tells us his dish is over-seasoned or just plain mediocre (see Chapter 6: The Lousy Beetroot Salad.), we'll do our best to work on it. It was our mistake, and we'll rectify it. However, if the same person gets upset because we stop him consuming outside food and beverages at our tables, or because we 'don't serve cuisines besides Middle Eastern', that's a gripe based solely on personal preference, and not one that I care to apologise for.

What I do is focus on the customers that are good for the restaurant. This might sound like discrimination, but you know what? The discrimination process already started long ago, when I decided on the kind of business I was setting up. If I'd chosen to operate a legit massage parlour, I'd have already axed every dude looking for a tsunami-special happy ending. Was my decision malicious? No! So I started getting comfortable with the idea that not everyone's feedback matters. There's no need to get worked up over criticism from those whom my brand is clearly not targeted at, or from someone who's much better off patronising someone else.

The ones that do matter are precious. They're the ones who come every other month, treat the staff with respect, abide by the house rules, bring along new friends, are an absolute pleasure to serve, and most important, truly derive value and satisfaction from what we were designed to provide. If I'd gone out of my way to change because unconstructive criticism from other customers got to me, then I'd risk losing these gems.

The moral of the story is: play your tiles right.

These guys looooove their smoked chicken (page 64).

My man Ming, who eats the same damn thing every time... (page 69).

SERVES 4

BRINE SOLUTION
½ lemon
1 bay leaf
1 sprig thyme
1 sprig rosemary
½ cup sea salt or kosher salt
½ cup brown sugar
5 cups water
5 cups ice

MARINADE
1 white onion, quartered
3 cloves garlic
1 tbsp turmeric powder
½ tbsp cumin powder
½ cup water
½ cup olive oil

1 chicken (1.2 to 1.5kg)
1 lemon, quartered into
    wedges, to serve
Toum, to serve (page 253)
Artichoke-style Pickles,
    to serve (page 257)

SPECIAL EQUIPMENT:
A meat thermometer

SMOKED CHICKEN
WITH PICKLES AND TOUM

This dish is a hot favourite, especially with regulars and friends, Howard Low and his wife Hui Nan (owners of Standing Sushi Bar and Tanuki Raw). It was inspired by all the meals I had in Lebanese charcoal roast chicken joints in Sydney, but we chose to smoke the chicken instead. Just because we can. To retain the Lebanese-y flavour of the dish, we serve the chicken with toum and pickles.

»»»»

To make the brine, place all the brining ingredients except the ice into a saucepan and bring to a boil to dissolve the salt and sugar. Remove from heat and stir in the ice, then pour the brine over the chicken. Allow the chicken to sit in the brine, fully submerged, for 6 to 8 hours.

To make the marinade, place all the marinade ingredients in a blender and blend till smooth. Rub this paste around and inside the chicken and leave to marinate for at least 6 hours; ideally overnight.

When ready to cook, hot smoke the chicken in a preheated hot smoker, until the internal temperature hits 77°C. You can measure this using a meat thermometer. The lower the ambient temperature and the longer you can smoke it, the better. If you'd rather roast it, preheat the oven to 140°C and roast the chicken for 40 to 50 minutes, until the internal temperature reaches 77°C. Allow to rest for 20 minutes before carving into thin slices a la Thanksgiving turkey, or into big pieces. It's all up to personal preference. Serve with lemon wedges, toum and pickles.

Meet Frankie,
Artichoke's meat man.

A NOTE ON HOT SMOKING

At Artichoke, we do our hot smoking in an ugly ghetto-style drum smoker. If you don't have a hot smoker at home, and don't mind putting in a bit of effort, you can smoke yours too. The Internet is bursting with instructions on how to set up a makeshift smoker at home. The principle is simple: cooking food over a combination of smouldering coals and wood smoke for flavour. You can do this in a simple kettle barbecue, with the lid covered. Make sure the coals and wood are close to ember stage before cooking the chicken, to prevent burning. (I recommend using apple or cherry wood in this case, as they won't overpower white meat. You may find these wood chips at barbecue supply stores.) Use a digital thermometer to gauge the internal temperature of the chicken—it's done when it reaches 77°C.

I'll leave you to further your research on DIY hot smoking. However, if you're a lazy ass punk (like me on my days off), rejoice in the fact that you can just chuck your bird in the oven and it'll still turn out pretty damn awesome. That said, whatever corners you choose to cut, do not omit the brining step. That's what makes the chicken tasty and juicy.

SMOKIN'

EAT
SLOPPILY

SMOKED SALMON PANCAKES

WITH BOURBON SOUR CREAM, WASABI PEA DUKKA AND HONEY

BOURBON SOUR CREAM

1 tbsp sour cream
1 tsp bourbon whiskey

WASABI PEA DUKKA

2½ tbsp wasabi peas, coarsely crushed in a pestle and mortar
½ tbsp white sesame seeds, toasted (page 19)

Clear honey, for drizzling
1 pancake (made from pre-mix)
1 handful finely shredded iceberg lettuce
2 tbsp egg mayo*
4 slices smoked salmon
A few thin slices of red onion, to garnish

*MAKING YOUR OWN EGG MAYO

Boil a couple of eggs for 10 minutes, then leave to cool. Peel and chop the hard-boiled eggs. Mix with ⅓ its perceived volume of mayonnaise (I go for the Kewpie brand every time). Add a pinch of freshly ground black pepper and you're done.

Ming Tan, chef of Lolla, loves this dish. The guy comes here and orders the same thing all the time—testament to how much of a 'dude' dish this is. We first served it at Dude Where's My Food (a week-long dinner event held during the 2013 F1 Singapore Grand Prix season) with the idea of combining and cohering the different associations with salmon on one plate. The Russians eat salmon on blini, so we used pancakes. The Japanese dip salmon into wasabi and soy sauce—we substituted with wasabi pea dukka. In a reference to a lox bagel, we added sour cream to the mix. And to make everything more dude-ish: Mr. Jack Daniels himself.

»»»»»

To make the sour cream, mix both ingredients together well.

To make the wasabi pea dukka, mix the ingredients together well.

Drizzle the honey over the pancake. Top with the lettuce and egg mayo. Lay the slices of smoked salmon over and sprinkle liberally with the dukka. Dollop the sour cream on top. Sprinkle with the red onion and drizzle with more honey.

SERVES
4*

2 cups cookie dough (page 248)
½ cup mini marshmallows
½ cup fresh raspberries
4 scoops gelato
(any flavour you desire)

*Makes 1 huge-ass cookie pie,
or 4 individual ones

COOKIE PIE

Michael McNab is one of my best fregulars (friend-regulars). One night, I gave him this dish to test out. He is Canadian, so I thought he'd appreciate a taste of home: comforting, warm, scoopable cookie dough with slightly crisp edges, and a dollop of ice cream. Guess what: the guy's eyes rolled back into his head as he took the first bite. When we served this dessert at Artichoke, the cookie changed every month. There were wasabi pea cookies, dried strawberry cookies, chocolate cookies, etc. Though this recipe refers to the Wasabi Pea and Caramelised White Chocolate Cookies (page 248), feel free to use any type of cookie dough you like.

»»»»

Preheat your oven to 180°C. Follow the instructions for making cookie dough in the Wasabi Pea and Caramelised White Chocolate Cookie recipe (page 248). Break the cookie dough into little nuggets that are approximately the size of MacDonald's chicken nuggets. Spread them across a large greased casserole or four individual ones. Ramekins will work too. (We use something called a cazuela at the restaurant, which is a shallow Spanish terracotta casserole.) Scatter marshmallows and raspberries around and on top of the dough nuggets to achieve a single flat layer chock-full of ingredients.

Bake the cookie pie(s) for 8 to 10 minutes, until the cookie dough melts down, engulfs the other ingredients, and starts to darken around the edges. Remove from the oven and immediately top with a scoop of gelato per person. Cookie dough tends to crisp up as it cools; what you're looking to do here is to eat it before it gets a chance to do that. Essentially, you should be eating a hot, molten 'pudding' of a cookie with crispy edges.

Comforting, warm, scoopable cookie dough with slightly crisp edges, and a dollop of ice cream.

What's So Difficult About That?

>>>>>>

CHAPTER 5

So you've heard me go on about how some customers get it while some others just don't. If we had a dollar for every time someone's said, "What's so difficult about that?" to us, we'd all have retired by now. Check out some of the things we've been grilled with:

The busy dude: "I've been waiting 10 minutes for my coffee. Does it really take that long to make a latte?"

The demanding lady: "Why can't you just make some poached eggs for me? How hard can it be to just boil some water and put two eggs in?"

The shouty schmuck: "Why do you keep saying you're fully booked? I see so many empty tables around… What the hell are you guys talking about?"

The group-who-shares-together-stays-together: "Why can't you cut our lamb burger into seven pieces for us to share? **What's so difficult about that?**"

We get these sorts of questions all the time. No kidding. Here are our replies, real and imagined.

To the busy dude

What we say as professionals:

"I'm so sorry, sir. Let us check on that for you. If there's any way I can speed it up, I'll do it. My apologies."

What we really wanna say as human beings:

"Seriously, dude, if you were the only person in here, you'd have received your coffee seven lifetimes ago. But if you'd take your eyes off my waitress's boobs for one second, you'll notice the other 45 people waiting for their hot drinks. It's a busy day, there's a queue, and you're somewhere in it. Chill out."

To the demanding lady

What we say as professionals:

"I'm sorry, ma'am, but we really can't do that. I hope you understand. Please, can I offer you something else?"

What we really wanna say as human beings:

"C'mon, lady, we're not stupid. We do know how to poach an egg. But there're 15 other tables' worth of nice people waiting patiently for their food right now, and we're busting our balls trying to feed everyone in decent time. There's no way we can pull one line cook off his station, dedicate another stove in the kitchen to simmering a pot of water, and deprive another six customers of their scrambled eggs in the meantime. Please order from the menu; it's there for a reason."

»»»»

»»»»

What we say as professionals:

"We're sorry, but those empty tables have been reserved. If you want, you are welcome to wait in our courtyard and we'll inform you once a table frees up. Please, sir, you don't have to raise your voice, we can hear you."

What we really wanna say as human beings:

"Dude, ever heard of reservations? And please calm the hell down if you even want to be served at all."

And to the group-who-shares-together-stays-together... »

600 g minced lamb

2 tbsp ras el hanout (page 30)

Salt and pepper

Olive oil, for frying

4 burger buns, each split into half

Vegetable oil, for frying

4 large eggs

Labneh Ranch Dressing,
   to garnish (page 262)

½ butter lettuce

¼ red onion, thinly sliced

Roasted Eggplant Relish,
   to garnish (page 263)

Dukka, to garnish (page 252)

LAMB BURGER

This is what happens when you attempt to slice something taller than it is wide into seven pieces. We were smacked with an online complaint for this, even after we acceded to their request. That said, do not be deceived by appearances. This burger is a simple and popular dish we served during Artichoke's teething, café-leaning stage.

》》》》》

Divide the lamb mince into four balls. Do not knead or mix the lamb mixture. Kneading it will only make it tough. Press these balls into flat rounds and sprinkle with the ras el hanout, salt and pepper on both sides. Heat up a grill or non-stick frying pan over medium-high heat and grease with the olive oil. Cook the lamb patties for several minutes on both sides till done to your liking. Again, this depends on many variables: how thick you like your patties, or whether you're cooking on a gas or induction stove. So don't be afraid to adjust as you go. I like my patties about 2cm thick and medium; that'll take roughly 2 minutes on each side plus 2 minutes of rest. However if you prefer thicker patties (3cm or more), cook them about 4 to 5 minutes on each side. When the patties are done, rest them in a warm place. In the meantime, toast your burger buns on the cut side in the same grill or pan you cooked your patties in.

If you feel that you can multi-task well, fry up the eggs sunny-side up while you toast the buns. Heat up the vegetable oil over high heat in a non-stick frying pan. Crack one egg in and cook till the whites get crispy around the edges but the yolk is still runny. Remove and repeat with the other eggs. Add more oil along the way if necessary.

Place the buns cut side up and smear on enough labneh ranch to satisfy you. Divide the lettuce and onion across the four burgers and top each with a lamb patty. Spoon some eggplant relish onto each patty and top with a fried egg. Sprinkle a little dukka over each egg and enclose the burger with the top half of the bun.

If you're a real burger guy like I am, you'll know that the only legit way to eat a burger is to squash it first. So get on it with your whole palm and press the shit out of the little bugger before you attempt to take a bite.

THAT'S WHAT'S SO DIFFICULT ABOUT THAT.

The Lousy Beetroot Salad

CHAPTER 6

This is the one story that's closest to my heart. I'll keep it short and sweet.

October 2010. Artichoke was two months old. I was in the kitchen slinging out brunch with my crew on a Saturday morning. One of the wait staff passed some feedback through the window—a girl at Table 2 thought our beetroot salad with shaved fennel, Valencia oranges and labneh was rather mediocre.

When I caught a break between orders, I went out and introduced myself, thanked her for her feedback, and reassured her that we'd look into improving it. The problem, we figured, was that the salad's components were disjointed. If you didn't combine everything in one mouthful, the intention and the fulsomeness of the dish would be lost.

True to my word, we worked on it. Instead of a salad, we created the beetroot 'tzatziki', layering the ingredients and flavours one on top of each other so that each forkful was like a standalone dish in itself. Till today, the dish is a crowd pleaser. The girl who set it on its right course is Roxanne, who now runs Overdoughs. At the end of 2014, she and I are getting married. Had my beetroot salad not sucked, things may not have worked out this way.

1 large beetroot,
  washed and scrubbed
2 tbsp olive oil
2 tbsp sherry vinegar
2 tbsp sugar
6 tbsp labneh (page 260)
½ tsp clear honey
A few sprigs of dill, chopped
Salt and pepper
Dukka, to garnish (page 252)
Extra virgin olive oil, for drizzling

BEETROOT TZATZIKI

WITH LABNEH AND DUKKA

Following Roxanne's comments on our beetroot salad, we wanted to create a beetroot-centric starter that offered all its flavours up in one mouthful. Working from the idea of a tzatziki—where cucumber, garlic, salt and olive oil are mixed into yoghurt—we chopped beetroot into bite-size pieces and folded them into labneh. Scattering the beetroot with an even coating of dukka added contrasting gravelly texture, its earthiness complementing the sweet beetroot well. Each spoonful would thus yield a harmony of sweet, salty and nutty flavours in the mouth. At Artichoke, we serve the dish as a mezze to be eaten with bread, but it goes great with chicken, lamb or fish mains too. As testament to how well-loved this dish is, we've not been able to remove it from our menu for over three years now.

»»»»

Preheat your oven to 200°C. Place the beetroot in a roasting pan and drizzle with the olive oil. Cover the pan with aluminium foil and roast for about 1 hour, or until the beetroot is tender. To test its doneness, pierce the beetroot with a wooden skewer. If there is any resistance at all, the beetroot is undercooked and should be roasted further. Remove from the oven and allow to cool for a bit. Peel and chop into small chunks of about 3cm each. While the pieces are still warm, marinate them in the sherry vinegar and sugar. Ideally, set aside for 3 hours or more.

To assemble, lift the beetroot pieces out of the marinating liquid. Place them in a bowl with the labneh, honey and dill. Mix well. Season to taste with salt and pepper. Place this mixture on a plate and sprinkle with the dukka. Drizzle with the extra virgin olive oil and serve.

Top: Beetroot Salad V.1;
bottom: Beetroot Salad V.2
aka Beetroot Tzatziki

¼ cup wild rice, cooked**
3 tbsp flaked almonds, toasted
   (page 19)
¼ cup coarse bulgur, soaked (page 17)
1 handful rocket, coarsely chopped
1 handful fresh mint, finely chopped
1 handful fresh coriander,
   finely chopped
2 small shallots, thinly sliced
3 tbsp pomegranate arils
Salt and pepper
4 tbsp Pomegranate Vinaigrette
   (page 256)
½ tbsp lemon juice
1 tbsp clear honey
2 tbsp extra virgin olive oil
2 tbsp Labneh Ranch Dressing
   (page 262) or thick Greek yoghurt

*As a side dish

FORGOTTEN GRAIN SALAD

Roxanne is one of the healthiest people I know; she could very well survive on hamster food for the rest of her life. Unsurprisingly, she loves this wholesome, fibre-rich salad. In Artichoke's version, we use a ton of grains that aren't really common (especially in Singapore), but are seeing a surge of popularity in recent years: quinoa, lentils, wild rice, black rice, bulgur, quinoa. In a way, the salad is an extension of a popular Turkish side dish called a kisir, which comprises bulgur, tomato paste, onion, garlic and chopped fresh herbs. This dish pops back on our menu occasionally, and is always a favourite. Here we present a simpler version for the home kitchen.

》》》》

Toss all the ingredients in a large mixing bowl except for the ranch dressing. Season to taste with salt and pepper, and adjust as you please with the pomegranate vinaigrette, lemon juice, honey, and extra virgin olive oil. Transfer to a large platter and top with a spoonful of ranch dressing.

**COOKING WILD RICE

Follow the manufacturer's instructions on the packet. A general rule of thumb is to cook 1 part wild rice in 3 parts water and a pinch of salt. Simmer for about 45 to 60 minutes in a covered pot, until the rice is tender and the kernels pop open. Drain off any excess liquid.

EAT
OTTOMANNISHLY

TURKISH-STYLE EGGPLANT

WITH TOMATO SMOOTHIE AND TAHINI YOGHURT

TOMATO SMOOTHIE

2 tbsp vegetable oil
2 shallots, chopped
2 cloves garlic, chopped
2 large tomatoes, chopped
¼ cup white wine
1 tsp smoked paprika
½ tsp sugar
½ cup water
Salt
½ cup extra virgin olive oil

Vegetable oil, for frying
1 large white onion, thinly sliced
Salt and pepper
1 large eggplant, about 30cm long
2 tbsp plain yoghurt
1 tbsp lemon juice
1 tsp tahini
1 tbsp pine nuts, toasted (page 19)
½ handful fresh coriander

The story goes that an Imam married the daughter of an olive oil merchant. She prepared this dish for him each night using the finest olive oil, but on the thirteenth night, she ran out of oil. When the Imam found out he wouldn't be having the dish that night, he fainted from shock.

This dish is based on a classic Turkish dish, 'Imam bayildi', which translates to 'the Imam (or religious leader) swooned'. It consists of a whole eggplant stuffed with onions, garlic and tomatoes, then simmered in olive oil. Our version here presents the eggplants in slices to facilitate sharing, and we've emulsified the tomatoes, spiking them with paprika to add a spicy, piquant dimension.

>>>>>

To make the smoothie, heat the oil over high heat in a small saucepan. Add the shallots and garlic and cook till slightly charred around the edges. Throw in the tomatoes and wine, reduce the heat to medium and cook for 5 to 6 minutes, until the tomatoes break down slightly. Stir in the smoked paprika, sugar and water. Cook for about 10 minutes more, or until the vegetables are soft. Season well with salt. Transfer the sauce into a blender and blend till smooth. With the motor running, open the hatch in the lid and slowly trickle in the olive oil to form an emulsion. The olive oil makes the sauce richer in texture. Once all the oil has been incorporated, re-season with salt if necessary and set aside at room temperature.

Oil the surface of a frying pan and heat over low-medium heat. Cook the onion slices for 30 to 45 minutes, until they caramelise and turn a deep brown. Keep stirring the onions to prevent them getting burnt. Season well with salt and pepper and set aside.

While the onions are being cooked, slice the eggplant crosswise into 2cm-thick rounds. Heat 5cm of vegetable oil in a heavy-based saucepan. When the oil is hot (you can tell when the surface starts to quiver), place the eggplant rounds into the oil in a single layer, and fry on both sides for 3 to 4 minutes in total, until the flesh turns golden-brown and soft. Fry them in batches, if necessary. Drain on kitchen paper, sprinkle with salt and set aside at room temperature.

To assemble, spread a layer of tomato smoothie on a serving plate. Place a layer of eggplant rounds on the plate and top each with a small mound of caramelised onions. Mix the yoghurt, lemon juice and tahini with a little salt and drizzle over the onions. Scatter with the pine nuts and coriander.

CHAPTER 7

Cuts & Burns

The people who choose to work in a kitchen, to subject themselves to the long hours and borderline inhuman conditions, have a genuine passion for food. They're also usually eccentric as hell.

These are people with major idiosyncrasies, some of whom would rather tweak micro greens for eternity than interact with other humans. Pair this with a job culture that prizes endlessly repetitive tasks, brute strength, and pure performance merit, and you get a system closely resembling a prison.

Just like in prison, battle scars here are worn with pride. The dysfunctional personalities existing in my professional sphere have a common characteristic: we kinda like pain. The deeper the cuts and the more severe the burns, the more legit we are among our peers. It's an unspoken thing within this subculture. Most of the time, cuts come from using the mandoline, seared forearms from grabbing stuff out of the oven, and general all-around burns from splattering oil.

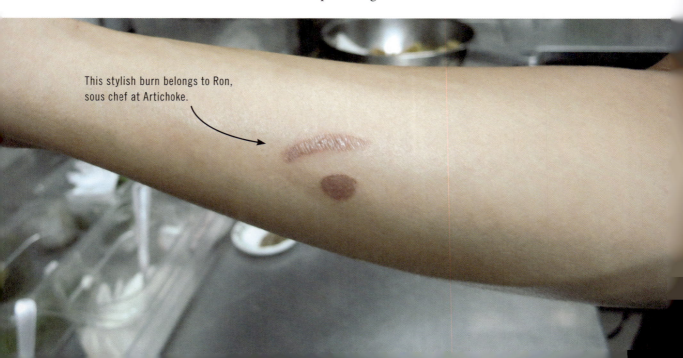

This stylish burn belongs to Ron, sous chef at Artichoke.

When I was an apprentice, I sliced off the tip of my right ring finger on a mandoline in the middle of a lunch slam. Like a true sick bastard, I retrieved the fingertip, adjusted it back on, strapped up the entire finger with masking tape, put on a latex glove and carried on working. Throughout the day, the glove kept filling up with blood and the head chef finally noticed. I got the rest of the day off. I didn't change the tape for a week out of fear that the fingertip would fall back off, so I just went to work with my mummified finger and a stack of gloves after that. Whaddayaknow? Two weeks later, the severed tip actually fused back on and my finger was as good as new.

Disclaimer: Please do not try this at home. If it happens to you, please, please seek professional medical treatment. I'm stressing professional.

I share this story with most other chefs I meet. Afterwards, I listen attentively while they tell me stories about how they once sliced their thumb right down to the bone, or how they had to wear an eye-patch like a pirate for a few days because of an oil-splatter burn to their eyeball. For us, trading injury stories is kinda like frat boys comparing cock size. Or girls comparing the price tags on their latest Birkins. Or banker-types at a VIP party, trading bonus figures.

The funny thing is, we seldom seek professional treatment for all this shit. I mean, that's what the first aid box is for, right? And the pharmacy right across the road? But we've got 20kg of fish to scale and gut, two cartons of spuds to peel, and half the population of this country to feed in 3 hours' time. There's just no time to queue up at the ER. Plus, why give up bragging rights or new self-medicating tips at our next chefs' meet-up?

Here are some recipes that involve high bodily risk. If you escape unscathed, you save yourself a load of unnecessary pain and end up with an awesome dish; if you get hurt in the process, you'll be able to give an awesome show-and-tell at your next night out (though if your friends aren't chefs themselves, they'll look at you like you've fucking lost it). Either way, you win.

The dysfunctional personalities existing in my professional sphere have a common characteristic: we kinda like pain.

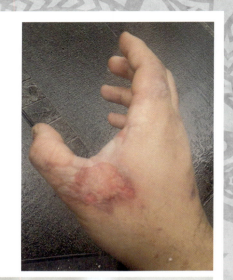

A Completely Gratuitous Gallery of Kitchen Burns, Cuts, Slices & Scrapes

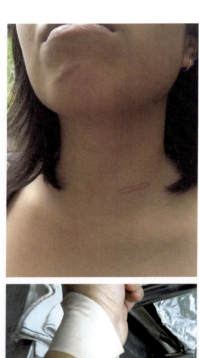

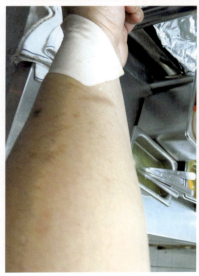

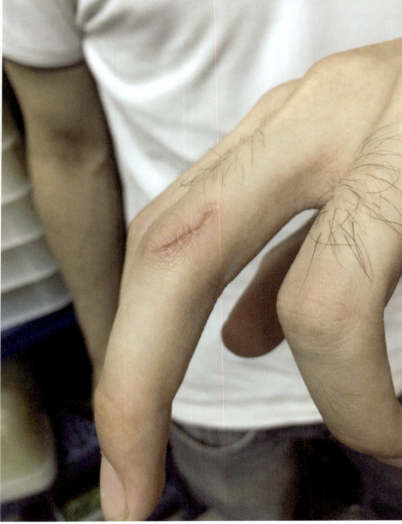

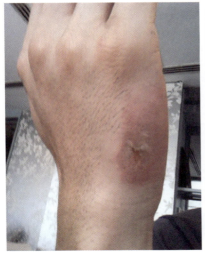
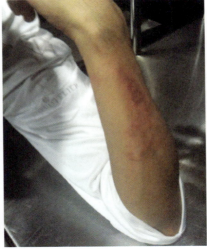
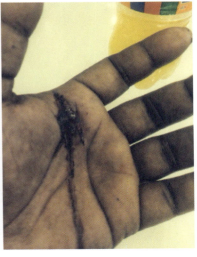
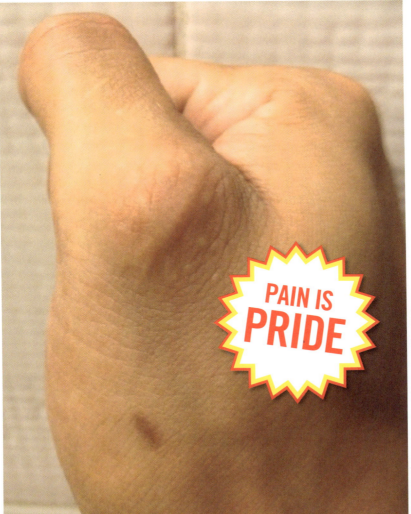

My chef friends from all over share their pain. (Facing page, clockwise from top): Jodin, oil splatter; Tim, knife nick; Jon, tiger-striped oven burns; Christine, neck burn from sliding oven tray. (This page, clockwise from top left): Benedict, steam oven scald; Joab, salamandar burn; Anpalagan, oyster shucking injury; Tyler, lopped off fingertip and nail; Jachin, oil burn.

PAIN IS PRIDE

THEY SPIT
LIKE A
BITCH

2 cups vegetable oil, for frying

½ white onion, thinly sliced

4 large prawns or 8 medium prawns,
    de-veined and butterflied

Salt and pepper

½ cup heavy cream

1 tbsp lemon juice

2 tbsp Green Chilli Harissa (page 253)

1 handful fresh coriander

1 small shallot, thinly sliced into rings

Lemon wedges, to serve

A few pieces of flatbread to serve
    (optional, page 18)

SIZZLING PRAWNS
WITH GREEN HARISSA CREAM, FRIED ONIONS AND CORIANDER

Just so you know, tiger prawns spit like a bitch while cooking. Any ingredient with a moisture build-up, encased within a crust or shell, will splatter on high heat. Leaving the shell on while cooking is important though, as it imparts a delicious charred, caramelised-prawn sweetness back into the meat and into the green harissa cream.

»»»»

To make the fried onions, heat the vegetable oil in a shallow saucepan or deep frying pan. When the oil is hot (i.e. it starts to smoke), add the onions in small batches and fry till brown and crispy. Drain on kitchen paper. Reserve 3 tablespoons of the oil, which should now be rich with a savoury onion fragrance. You can strain the remaining oil and reserve it for other dishes.

Heat up the 3 tablespoons of onion oil in a large frying pan or heavy cast-iron pan over high heat. When the pan is very hot, lay the prawns in one layer in the pan and sprinkle with a pinch of salt. Cook for 1 minute on one side. Flip the prawns and cook for another minute, then add in the cream, lemon juice and harissa. Stir well and allow to sizzle for a minute more, or until the prawns are cooked through. Season the sauce to taste with salt and pepper.

Moving quickly, remove the pan from the stove and garnish the prawns with a mini-mountain of fried onions, coriander, shallots and lemon wedges. Present the entire pan to your guests while it's still sizzling for maximum style points. Serving this dish with flatbread is quite a brilliant idea. You and your guests will be wiping the sauce out of that pan like a bunch of unrestrained 6-year-olds going to town on an unmanned candy shop.

TOASTED SEMOLINA PUDDING

100 g fine semolina
2 tbsp unsalted butter
2 shallots, finely chopped
500 ml full cream milk,
    plus additional for adjusting
1 cup mascarpone cheese
100 g feta cheese, finely crumbled
Salt and pepper

ANCHOVY CRUMBS

2 tbsp salted butter,
    plus additional for adjusting
2 fillets salted anchovies
1 cup coarse breadcrumbs or panko
½ clove garlic, finely chopped

Fresh herbs (basil, mint, dill, etc.),
    roughly torn, to garnish
Extra virgin olive oil

*If you thought hot oil splatters were nasty, wait till you get hit by flying semolina lava—the napalm of the food world. Hot oil and water burns are mild in comparison because they spread out and cool almost instantly. Semolina mixtures, on the other hand, are thick and hold an Energizer bunny's worth of heat; they cling to your skin upon impact, refusing to spread out or slide off. To save yourself some hurt, wear long sleeves and use a lid as a shield while you stir the pot. Or just get someone else to do this for you.

TOASTED SEMOLINA PUDDING

WITH FETA AND ANCHOVY CRUMBS

I've always been obsessed with mash-like food that isn't actually mash, like grits or polenta. Enter semolina, a coarse flour made from durum wheat. You'll find it in Mediterranean desserts such as basbousa (cooked semolina soaked in syrup) and galaktoboureko, a Greek semolina custard pie. I wanted to experiment with a savoury version, so I whipped semolina in hot milk to make a thick savoury pudding. Toasting the grains before cooking would also impart a warm, nutty flavour akin to breakfast cereal. This pudding is great with roasted meats and rich meat stews. Try this with our smoked chicken (page 64) or Lambgasm (page 119).

»»»»

To make the semolina pudding, toast the semolina in a dry pan over medium heat for 3 to 5 minutes, until slightly golden-brown. Set aside. Heat the butter over medium heat in a saucepan and cook the shallots for 5 to 7 minutes, until soft and sweet. Add the milk and bring to a boil. Whisk in the semolina gradually. It will thicken up on contact with the milk and the mixture will begin to bubble and spit dangerously*. After 5 minutes, the mixture should look like molten lava from the earth's core. Turn off the heat then fold in the mascarpone and feta. At this point, the texture of the pudding should resemble a thick custard. If it's too thick, add more hot milk to loosen it up. Season to taste with salt and pepper. To keep the pudding creamy, keep it warm by transferring it into a mixing bowl sitting over a pot of hot water.

To make the anchovy crumbs, heat the butter over medium-high heat in a frying pan and add the anchovy fillets. Break up the fillets with a fork and allow to dissolve into the butter. Toss in the breadcrumbs and garlic. Add more butter as necessary to saturate the breadcrumbs. You'll know the breadcrumbs are hitting saturation point when any butter being added isn't absorbed by the crumbs. Fry till the breadcrumbs turn golden-brown and crispy. Drain on kitchen paper and allow to cool. The breadcrumbs can be kept for up to 2 days in an airtight container.

To serve, spoon the pudding into a shallow dish and scatter the anchovy crumbs over it. Garnish with the herbs and a drizzle of oil.

CRISPY TARO 'KATAIFI'

1 small taro or yam
Vegetable oil, for deep-frying
Salt and pepper

TUNA 'KIBBEH NAYEH'

2 tbsp fine bulgur (page 17)
  or instant couscous
2 tbsp hot water
400 g sashimi-grade tuna,
  chopped into 1 to 2cm cubes
1 clove garlic, finely chopped
1 medium shallot, thinly sliced
1 spring onion, thinly sliced
½ handful fresh mint leaves,
  thinly sliced
2 tbsp light soya sauce (optional)
2 tbsp extra virgin olive oil
1 tsp white pepper
1 tsp baharat (page 255)
Sea salt

Extra virgin olive oil, for drizzling
4 lemon wedges
Nori harissa, to serve
  (optional, page 231)
Labneh Ranch Dressing, to serve
  (optional, page 262)

The danger in this dish
derives from the taro 'kataifi',
our version of Levantine
shredded filo pastry. Many a
hand has been sliced; many a
fingertip nicked in the process
of julienning a taro on a
mandoline. Be careful,
and go slow.

TUNA 'KIBBEH NAYEH'

WITH CRISPY TARO KATAIFI

Kibbeh nayeh is the Levantine's answer to a meat tartare, with the addition of spices and bulgur wheat. It can be made with either ground lamb or beef. Our version is a riff on tradition, using fish instead of meat; and we've topped it with a bunch of crispy taro flakes for a texture explosion. Feel free to use any other sashimi-grade fish that you fancy, such as salmon, kingfish or swordfish.

》》》》

To make the crispy taro strings, peel the taro and slice it on a mandoline into thin strips. Preheat the oil in a deep fryer to 180°C. If you don't have a deep fryer, heat 10cm of vegetable oil in a deep pot or saucepan over high heat till it reaches 180°C. When the oil is hot enough, deep-fry the taro till golden and crispy throughout. Season generously with salt and pepper while still hot. Leave to cool on absorbent paper. You can make your taro strings up to 3 days ahead and keep them stored in an airtight container.

To make the 'kibbeh nayeh', soak the bulgur in the hot water for 5 minutes. Drain off excess water. Add the tuna to a mixing bowl along with the bulgur and all the remaining ingredients. Mix well. Season to taste with sea salt.

Serve the 'kibbeh nayeh' on a large platter, or divide it across four serving plates. Sprinkle the top with the taro 'kataifi' then drizzle with additional extra virgin olive oil if you like. Serve with lemon wedges, and a bowl each of nori harissa and labneh ranch to pass around the table.

> " Cuts come from using the mandoline, seared forearms from grabbing stuff out of the oven, and general all-around burns from splattering oil. "

DANGER

CHAPTER 8

Reckless Creativity

»»»»

Did you know that frozen olive oil looks exactly like lemon sorbet? This is a fact I exploited in university, when a couple of jokester friends and I froze the oil in a couple of ramekins, poured some apple cordial on top to mask the smell, and handed them innocently to the girls who lived downstairs. Needless to say, they were really pissed.

We each had to down a shot of pure olive oil in front of them as a conciliatory gesture, but the damage had been done. Boo-yah.

One could describe our prank as recklessly creative, and it's manifested in our approach at Artichoke and Overdoughs. Reckless creativity has always been a cornerstone of our style, essentially summing up what we stand for: not to take ourselves too seriously.

One person who played a huge part in propelling us in this direction is **Kel**, ex-sous chef at Artichoke and now head chef at Overdoughs. Like me, he is one sick, twisted bastard. When two sick, twisted bastards are thrown together in a high-pressure environment, shit ensues. We egg each other on, percolating stupid ideas and birthing hypothetical scenarios into the unforgiving light of day. "Let's beer-batter chicken, wrap it in strip upon strip of bacon, and deep-fry it," he would say.

"Let's soak it in maple syrup after," I'd continue.

It's probably fair to say that we do things as much for shits and giggles as for professional culinary pride. When we brainstorm dishes, there's no stopping us from unleashing our wildest ideas.

When two sick, twisted bastards are thrown together in a high-pressure environment, shit ensues.

This is Junhao, previously head baker at Overdoughs. He is also a sick bastard.

Timeline Photos

Back to Album · Artichoke cafe & bar's photos · Artichoke cafe & bar's Page   Previous · Next

CHALLENGE BJORN:
Wipe the smiles off those faces!

Like | Comment

 Artichoke cafe & bar
You guys ready for another challenge? Throw ingredients at us for the next round of Challenge Bjorn! We're looking for another brunch dish this time.

Here's what you need to do:
Throw us 3 ingredients at most. We'll choose 1 ingredient from 3 people and create a brand new brunch dish. If your ingredient is chosen, you get to come for brunch and enjoy the dish you helped to create for free.

Remember, stay away from generic ingredients (garlic, rice, chicken, etc.). Get creative. Come at us!

TWO BLOOMIN' IDIOTS

A Christmas Double Down (two pieces of fried chicken wrapped around honey-glazed ham with a candy cane stuck on top) and a belly bacon birthday cake with mayonnaise-based text embellishment.

"If you're going to die tomorrow," I constantly challenge Kel, "what nasty-ass shit would you come up with today?" In true Artichoke/Overdoughs spirit, he would grab the challenge by the balls and own it, rolling out chocolate tarts with cheese-flavoured Doritos, Jack Daniel's fudge and Skittles. Or crispy chicken skin donuts with smoked paprika Pop Rocks... y.ou get the picture. Sometimes these dishes aren't even vaguely Middle Eastern. But we serve them anyway, without regard for consequences, simply 'cause they're sick. Plus, we have some awesome regulars/taste-testers we love to force this shit upon. It doesn't always work. Whenever things flop, we just stand back and have a good laugh at the disaster. No ingredient is too lowbrow, no combination too insane.

For a while, we ran a 'Challenge Bjorn' campaign on our Facebook page where the public could suggest ideas for ingredients for our next dish. Depending on the size of our cojones at the time, we picked ingredients with varying degrees of whackiness and combined them to create a dish.

Here are a couple of past examples:

Beef tongue + Chinese haw flakes + nachos = Pan-seared beef tongue steaks with haw flake molasses, crushed nachos and braised cabbage (page 102).

Fried chicken + peanut butter + marshmallows + Sriracha = **The Donut Zinger**, a peanut butter frosting-glazed donut sandwich, studded with marshmallows and hundreds-and-thousands. We spread a garlic-marshmallow fluff on the bottom, stuffed the donut-sandwich with fried chicken, and served it with Sriracha coleslaw.

The real challenge was actually including the Franken-dish in our menu for at least a weekend. Some dishes played a little more safe and sold well; a couple even stayed on the menu for a long time (e.g. **Bacon Sweet Potato Hash with Fried Eggs and Bourbon Butter**, page 161). Others were totally trippy and came up short in the sales department. The weekend we put the Donut Zinger on our brunch menu, everyone had a good laugh reading the description, but no one actually ordered it. We ultimately wasted 15kg of chicken, 40 peanut butter-frosted donuts, two jars of garlic-marshmallow fluff and mounds of Sriracha coleslaw; but watching customers crack up upon reading the menu made it all worth it.

Goz Lee, good friend and author of *Plusixfive: A Singaporean Supper Club Cookbook*, once described me as 'unhinged'. High five. I'll take that as a compliment. Here are some unhinged recipes.

"If you're going to die tomorrow," I constantly challenge Kel, "what nasty-ass shit would you come up with today?"

SEASONED WHITEBAIT FLOUR

½ cup corn flour
½ cup rice flour
1 tsp chilli powder
1 tsp smoked paprika
1 tsp salt, plus additional for
seasoning the fried whitebait
1 tsp white pepper

Vegetable oil, for deep-frying
400 g whitebait
2 tsp sumac (page 17)
Small block of Manchego
or any other firm cheese
(such as Parmesan, pecorino, etc.)
Saffron Mayo, to serve (page 255)
Pomegranate Ketchup,
to serve (page 256)

You'll notice we add sumac,
instead of lemon juice, to the
fried whitebait because sumac
bestows a sour tang without
wetting the batter. You may
use lemon juice instead of
sumac, but do expect it to
soften the crust a little.

FISH FRIES
WITH SAFFRON MAYO AND POMEGRANATE KETCHUP

**Fries with ketchup and mayo: a classic, perfect for messing
around with. Frankie, one of my chefs, and I came up with a
logical parallel: instead of potatoes, we'd use whitebait. (It has
a similar shape, and fries up nicely.) Instead of tomato ketchup,
we'd use a similarly tangy pomegranate version. And mayo is
so 2005... so we spiked it with saffron for some Middle Eastern
street cred. Feel free to go nuts with the shaved cheese on
top—don't pay any attention to the purists who tell you fish
and cheese don't mix.**

»»»»»

To make the seasoned whitebait flour, mix all the ingredients
well in a bowl.

Preheat the oil in a deep fryer to 180°C. If you do not have a deep
fryer, heat 10cm of oil in a deep pot or saucepan over high heat
till it reaches 180°C. When the oil is hot enough, toss the whitebait
well in the seasoned batter and allow to rest for 1 to 2 minutes.
(This is the part of the recipe that's crucial to making this simple
dish great. Allowing the fish to sit in the flour creates a thicker layer
of batter such that it doesn't break and fall off while frying.) Place
the whitebait in a colander with large holes and shake off the excess
batter. Place into the hot oil and do not mess with the fish. Let the
little fishies cook, people. Messing with them now breaks the fragile
crust before it has had the chance to form. Fry for 3 minutes, or
until the batter turns a deep gold. Remove from the oil and toss
immediately with the sumac and a pinch more of salt. Place on
a plate and shave as much cheese as you want all over the fish.
Serve with the mayo and ketchup as dips.

FALAFEL-BATTERED FISH NUGGETS
WITH POTATO CHIP TABBOULEH

480 g white fish fillets (such as snapper,
  cod, haddock, whiting, etc.), skinned
  and with pin bones removed
Salt
Plain flour, for dredging
Vegetable oil, for deep-frying

FALAFEL BEER BATTER
½ cup canned chickpeas
330 ml beer, chilled (I like using pale
  ales, but feel free to use whatever
  you wish)
115 g plain flour
1 tsp cumin powder
1 tsp paprika
1 medium green chilli, finely chopped
1 clove garlic, finely chopped
1 handful fresh coriander,
  finely chopped
½ tbsp lemon juice
Salt

TABBOULEH DRESSING
1 tbsp lemon juice
½ clove garlic, finely chopped
¼ tsp allspice
¼ tsp cinnamon powder
1 tsp sumac (page 17)
½ cup extra virgin olive oil
Salt and pepper

POTATO CHIP TABBOULEH
1 large tomato,
  de-seeded, finely chopped
⅛ red onion, finely chopped
1 stalk spring onion, thinly sliced
1 cup fresh mint, finely chopped
1 cup fresh parsley, finely chopped
1 large bag potato chips

Labneh Ranch Dressing,
  to serve (page 262)
Lemon wedges, to serve

As you've probably intimated by now, Artichoke's philosophy can be loosely described as Middle Eastern influence meets fresh artisanal ingredients meets dude food attack. This dish is an apt illustration. Haziz (ex-sous chef at Artichoke) and I wanted to have fun with the tired idea of fish and chips. We incorporated the flavours of falafel into the fish, replacing breadcrumbs with ground chickpeas and drawing in the Middle Eastern profiles of cumin, coriander, garlic and paprika. The chips were a eureka moment—we thought, what if chips and salad were combined? (It probably helped that we were lazy-ass dudes always on the lookout for a shortcut.) The idea for a potato chip tabbouleh reared its head. We replaced the traditional bulgur with crushed, good quality potato chips that would retain their crispness even after dressing. I recommend going for more premium brands with thicker cuts, such as Red Rock Deli, Kettle Chips and, funnily enough, Calbee Jagabee.

>>>>>

Cut the fish fillets into fingers about the size and shape of your, well, index finger. Season with some salt on both sides. Coat evenly with the flour and set aside.

To make the beer batter, chop the chickpeas in a food processor till they resemble coarse breadcrumbs. Do not chop them too finely. In a mixing bowl, whisk the beer into the flour, then add the chickpeas and the remaining ingredients. Season well with salt.

Preheat the oil in a deep fryer to 180°C. If you do not have a deep fryer, heat 10cm of vegetable oil in a deep pot or saucepan over high heat till it reaches 180°C. Dip the floured fish fingers into the beer batter, then deep-fry for 3 to 4 minutes, until they turn golden-brown. Drain well and keep warm.

To make the tabbouleh dressing, whisk all the ingredients together, and season to taste with salt and pepper.

To make the tabbouleh, first drain the tomato of excess juice. Toss all the ingredients, except for the potato chips, in a large mixing bowl. Coat liberally with the tabbouleh dressing. Grab the bag of chips and smash it around violently. What you wanna do is crush the shit of out the stuff inside. (Tip: Opening the bag to let out excess air leads to more efficient crushing.) Add the entire portion of crushed chips to the mixing bowl and toss once more. Serve alongside the fish nuggets, labneh ranch and lemon wedges.

The poster for our gnarly, one week only event.

TONGUE STEAKS

1 beef tongue
1 cup white wine
1 white onion, halved
2 bay leaves
2 sprigs thyme
2 tsp salt

HAW FLAKE MOLASSES

5 packets haw flakes
   (Sunflower Brand), finely chopped
5 tbsp water, plus additional
   for diluting
1 tbsp brown sugar
1 tsp lemon juice

BRAISED CABBAGE

4 tbsp olive oil
4 cloves garlic, finely chopped
½ white onion, finely chopped
½ red cabbage, sliced
1 cup red wine vinegar
½ cup white sugar
Salt

1 tbsp olive oil or unsalted butter,
   for frying
Salt and pepper
Japanese mayo, for drizzling
   (Kewpie brand, optional)
1 cup tortilla chips,
   coarsely crushed (go with
   your favourite brand and
   flavour—I'm a Doritos fan
   all the way)
1 handful fresh herbs
   (such as parsley, mint,
   tarragon, basil, dill, etc.),
   to serve

BEEF TONGUE STEAKS

WITH HAW FLAKE MOLASSES, NACHOS AND BRAISED CABBAGE

A 'Challenge Bjorn' dish. Goz, whom I didn't know at the time, goaded me on Facebook to use haw flakes in a recipe. "Dude, are you man enough?" I believe he said. "You got the balls to pull this off? I'll salute you if you do!" Well, evidently I did, and I raised the stakes by throwing in beef tongue. What do you say now, Goz?

Beef tongue can be found at a good, Euro-centric butcher, such as Swiss Butchery or Huber's Butchery. This recipe also calls for packets of haw flakes, by which I mean the standard pink-and-green-wrapped stacks of Sunflower Brand haw discs. Every Singaporean child should know what these look like. If you don't, there's always Google.

»»»»

To prepare the tongue, place the whole fugly-looking thing in a large pot along with the other ingredients. Pour in water till everything is just submerged. Bring to a gentle simmer for 2 to 3 hours, until the tongue is tender throughout. You know the tongue is done when a small paring knife can slide in and out of the flesh without much resistance. Any significant resistance is a sign you need to keep simmering. Transfer the cooked tongue to a bowl of ice water and discard everything else. Allow to cool for 10 minutes, then peel away the outer skin. It should come away very easily. Trim off any large veins and other nasty-looking stuff at its base before slicing the rest of the meat into 1cm-thick slabs.

To make the haw flake molasses, add the haw flakes and water to a saucepan. Whisk over medium heat, adding more water a little at a time to dissolve the haw flakes. When the flakes are fully dissolved, add in as much brown sugar and lemon juice to your liking. You do not need to use the specified amount in the ingredient list. The final product should be sweet and very slightly sour. Continue to boil until it reaches the consistency of a thin syrup. Allow to cool.

To make the braised cabbage, heat the olive oil over medium-high heat in a large saucepan or wok. Add the garlic and onions and fry till fragrant. Add in the cabbage, vinegar and sugar and continue to cook, covered, for 10 minutes more, or until the cabbage just starts to become tender. Season to taste with salt.

Challenge Accepted

Challenge Bjorn #3:

- Ox tongue

- Nachos

- Haw flakes

Like   Comment

Artichoke cafe & bar
Here it is. You guys threw us an epic challenge, and we, in turn had to Level Up. Challenge Bjorn #3 for dinner: beef tongue, haw flakes and nachos - grilled beef tongue, red cabbage escabeche, haw flake molasses, doritos & kewpie.

Officially on our dinner menu from tonight, a hearty serving of irony - these mad-as-shit ingredients served in the daintiest way.

To complete the dish, heat the remaining tablespoon of olive oil in a non-stick frying pan. When the pan starts smoking, sear the tongue slices on both sides for about 2 minutes each. Season to taste with salt and pepper as the slices are searing.

To serve, place a mound of cabbage on a platter and top with the tongue slices. Drizzle with the **haw flake** molasses and Japanese mayo. Scatter a handful of crushed tortilla chips over the top and garnish with the fresh herbs.

EAT LIKE A PORN STAR

You may garnish the dish with chopped chives, spring onions, popcorn, assorted processed junk food, etc. Or do like the Aussies and finish with a huge squirt of ketchup.

BACON HOTDOG PIES

400 g thick-cut belly bacon, chopped into 2cm cubes

2 cloves garlic, finely chopped

1 large white onion, finely chopped

1 stick celery, finely chopped

4 large sausages, roughly chopped (preferably a nice pork bratwurst or a frankfurter)

1 tbsp plain flour

1 cup chicken stock

1 tbsp yellow mustard

1 tsp curry powder

Salt and pepper

4 sheets standard frozen puff pastry, just thawed

Vegetable oil or unsalted butter, for greasing pie moulds

1 egg, beaten

Extra grilled sausages, for 'garnish'

TIGER BEER CHEESE SOUP

2 tbsp plain flour

2 tbsp butter

1 clove garlic, finely chopped

1 330ml bottle Tiger Beer or any other beer of your choice

1½ cup chicken or vegetable stock

½ cup heavy cream

2 cups cheddar cheese, grated

Salt and pepper

BACON HOTDOG PIE
WITH TIGER BEER CHEESE SOUP

Imagine a flaky, oozy, greasy meat pie, sitting pretty in a bowl of thick, creamy soup and topped with ketchup. Man-food for generations past and generations to come, in all its primitive glory. How much better can it get? The Aussies have nailed it: for the uninitiated, this is the Pie Floater. Here's our take on the dish, with some Singaporean swagger in the way of curry powder and Tiger Beer. Who knew life could be this sweet? You can find thick-cut belly bacon from good Euro-centric butchers, such as Swiss Butchery and Huber's Butchery.

»»»»»

To make the pie filling, fry the bacon in a heavy-bottomed pot or casserole over medium heat till golden-brown. Add the garlic, onion and celery and fry till tender and translucent. Add the sausages and flour to the pot and cook for 1 minute more. Add in the chicken stock, mustard and curry powder and bring to a simmer. Stir constantly for 5 minutes, or until the mixture thickens and starts to look like thick KFC mashed potato gravy. Season to taste with salt and pepper and allow to cool to room temperature.

In the meantime, preheat your oven to 180°C. Cut out circles of puff pastry large enough to line the bases and sides of four 9cm round pie moulds. Cut out more circles for the pie 'lids' and set aside. Grease the moulds with the oil and line them with the pastry, then spoon the filling in. Top each pie with a lid, pinching the edges to seal in the filling. Brush the tops of the pies with the beaten egg, then bake the pies in the oven for 30 minutes.

For fun (and phallic) presentation, I like to cut out a hole in the top of my pies and poke half a grilled sausage in (see picture).

To make the soup, combine the flour, butter and garlic in a heavy-bottomed pot. Cook over low heat for 1 minute or until the mixture turns golden. Add in the beer and mix well. Bring to a boil for half a minute, then reduce to a simmer for 5 minutes, to burn off the alcohol. Add the stock and cream and simmer for 10 minutes more. Remove the pot from the stove and whisk in the cheese. Season to taste with salt and pepper. Pour the soup over the pies to serve.

400 g calamari, cleaned
4 tbsp zhoug (page 262)
Zest of 1 lemon
3 tbsp olive oil, plus additional
  for brushing the calamari
½ cup Rice Krispies
1 tsp smoked paprika
Salt and pepper
1 handful mixed salad leaves
2 to 3 tbsp Pomegranate Vinaigrette
  (page 256)
Saffron Mayo, to garnish (page 255)
Extra virgin olive oil, for drizzling
Lime wedges, to serve

BBQ CALAMARI
WITH ZHOUG, SAFFRON MAYO AND RICE KRISPIES

We took elements of paella—rice, seafood, saffron—and twisted them around to make this dish. To make it more 'Artichokey', we marinate the calamari in zhoug, a Yemeni green spice paste. It's then tossed with saffron-spiked mayo, while the nod to 'rice' comes in the form of Rice Krispies, sprinkled on top for a nice finishing crunch.

»»»»

If you're using whole calamari, cut the body into thick rings and leave the tentacles whole. Marinate the calamari pieces in the zhoug, lemon zest and 1 tbsp of olive oil for 4 to 6 hours. Meanwhile, toast the Rice Krispies in a pan over medium heat for 2 to 3 minutes with the remaining olive oil and the smoked paprika. The Krispies should turn golden brown and even a little charred around the edges. Season to taste with salt and pepper, then leave to dry on kitchen paper.

Preheat your ridged stovetop grill or barbecue. If you're using a ridged stovetop grill, turn it on to high heat. If you're using a charcoal barbecue, which I would definitely suggest, wait till the coals have burnt down to glowing embers. Grill the calamari for 1 to 2 minutes on each side, brushing occasionally with more olive oil. Season well with salt and pepper. Leave them on a little longer if using the barbecue. The calamari is done when they turn from translucent to opaque. Pull them off the fire and let them cook a little further in their residual heat.

Quickly toss the salad leaves with the vinaigrette. Top the calamari with a lashing of mayo and serve alongside the salad. Finish the dish with a scattering of toasted Rice Krispies, a drizzle of extra virgin olive oil and some lime wedges.

MAKES 4 SANDWICHES

CHAR SIEW BAO GRILLED CHEESE SANDWICHES

4 large char siew baos
  (Chinese roast pork buns)
½ cup Sichuan chye
  (Sichuan preserved vegetables),
  thinly sliced
Freshly ground black pepper
2 cups shredded cheese mix
  (any combination of mozzarella,
  Gouda, Parmesan, red cheddar,
  Monterey Jack, etc.)
Olive oil, for frying
Sriracha sauce or any other bottled
  garlic chilli sauce, to serve

One night, a while ago, I woke up with this fully formed thought: what would happen if I made a grilled cheese sandwich out of a char siew bao (Chinese roast pork bun), essentially a sandwich with the meat built in? I got out of bed at 5am, drove to the nearest convenience store, purchased the last slightly crusty bao languishing in their steamer, came right home, split it in half, stuffed it ridiculously with cheese, and pressed the shit out of it in my panini press. IT TASTED GREAT. We've served it since at events, including one at the Asian Civilisations Museum and the Hermès Games Singapore. Here's to so-bad-it's-good ideas.

While I'd recommend getting large char siew baos from a good quality vendor (e.g. Teck Kee Pau), there are no issues obtaining them from the hot box in your friendly neighbourhood 7/11 or gas station. Just don't ask the clerk how long they've been sitting there for. You really don't wanna know.

>>>>>

Pop the buns straight in the fridge and allow them to cool completely. Once cold, slice them in half crosswise as if they were burger buns. Divide the Sichuan chye across the 4 bun 'bases' and sprinkle with a pinch of black pepper.

Now for the cheese. You can use a single type of cheese if you can't be bothered to get a mix. But if you want to go all-out-gourmet (and because it really is worth the effort), then go with my suggested ratio of equal parts mozzarella, red cheddar and Parmesan. Mozzarella is nice and elastic; cheddar is creamy; Parmesan gives a good salty kick. Divide the cheese across each 'base' and pop on the top bun to get what essentially looks like a **very messy sandwich**.

To simulate a panini press, grease a non-stick frying pan with the olive oil and fry the sandwiches over low heat with a weight on top. For a DIY cooking weight, you can use a brick wrapped in aluminum foil, or a pot filled with water and whose base is lined with aluminum foil. Remember to oil the foil so that it does not stick to your sandwich. Flip the sandwiches over when they are golden-brown on the bottom and continue to cook till the tops are golden-brown too. If you have a panini press like I do, you can save yourself the trouble of weighing them down and flipping. Just grill these suckers George Foreman-style.

When done, they should be shatteringly crispy on the outside and melty-gooey-cheesy on the inside. Dip in Sriracha sauce and chow down.

Have a good laugh at how you've just disrespected generations of tradition and made something totally stupid out of something so traditional.

EAT
AGGRESSIVELY

NACHO 'HUMMUS'

2 grab-fuls of your favourite
   tortilla chips (I love Doritos'
   Taco Flavoured Tortilla Chips)
2 cups chicken stock or water,
   plus additional for adjusting
1 clove garlic, finely chopped
½ tbsp lemon juice
1 tsp smoked paprika
½ cup extra virgin olive oil
Salt and pepper

400 g beef or lamb sausages
Vegetable oil or olive oil, for frying
1 red onion, finely chopped
1 clove garlic, finely chopped
2 large green chillies or
   1 green capsicum, thinly sliced
1 tsp chilli flakes
Dash of lemon juice (optional)
1 handful fresh coriander, roughly torn
1 stalk spring onion, finely chopped

Smoked Tomato Ezme,
   to serve (page 257)
Sour cream, to serve
More crushed tortilla chips, to garnish

Disclaimer: With all this talk
of grits, why am I calling this
dish a 'hummus'? Well, I have
to stick to my Artichoke guns.
Also, hummus and grits have
a similar texture. Kinda.

NACHO 'HUMMUS'
WITH SPICY SAUSAGE AND TOMATO EZME

I have a sick fascination with nachos. When I have nothing to do, I eat them. It's like a hobby. One day, it occurred to me: what would happen if I broke the chips down to make a type of grits? Both of them are typically made from ground corn, so all I'd be doing is reverting the chips back to an earlier state. Un-processing processed food—why not? And to tie the idea of a nacho-inspired dish together, we added spicy sausages and tomato ezme as our version of chilli con carne.

〉〉〉〉〉

To make the 'hummus', chuck the chips into a blender and blitz them into a fine powder. Place in a heavy-based saucepan and add the chicken stock. Bring to a simmer, whisking constantly. If the mixture gets too dry, add more chicken stock to loosen it up. Once you've got it to the texture of pancake batter, whisk in the garlic, lemon juice and paprika. Simmer for 1 minute more, then whisk in the extra virgin olive oil and season well with salt and pepper. Set aside. The 'hummus' is served at room temperature, so do keep in mind that it will thicken and stiffen slightly as it cools. Before serving, you may need to whisk it with or without a little hot water to loosen it up to a spreadable consistency.

Remove the sausage meat from their casings. Heat up some vegetable oil in a non-stick frying pan over high heat. Add the sausage meat, breaking it up into a rough mince as you cook. When the mince is lightly browned, add the onion, garlic, chillies and chilli flakes. Keep tossing and cooking for 3 minutes more, or until the vegetables are slightly soft. Add a dash of lemon juice and remove from the heat. Mix in the coriander and spring onion.

To assemble, spread the 'hummus' on the base of a communal plate and top with the sausage-onion mix. Finish with a few dollops each of ezme and sour cream, then sprinkle with more crushed chips.

The Lambgasm

>>>>>

The Lambgasm is, hands down, Artichoke's signature dish. About six months after opening, we decided it was time to put something too big for our own good on the menu. Essentially we wanted to stick a middle finger to lamb chops or pork chops or ribs—the neat, ubiquitous, common, sterile option on most restaurant menus. Those were nice, yet boring. We wanted to throw caution to the wind; test our diners' tolerance; put out something challenging. And what was challenging was an entire lamb shoulder, served steaming and whole at the table with pickles, condiments and bread.

It would be an amazing large format dish that could feed 2 to 12 people, depending on the ability of their stomachs to distend. It would also be another fantastic way for people to engage with the food and each other. In true sick bastard spirit, we still serve the lamb with a knife stuck straight in, like it was a beast we just hunted down. Truth be told, the knife is mainly theatrical: the meat is so soft that it falls away at the slightest prodding with a pair of tongs (which we also provide). We encourage people to hack at the slab of meat on the table, rip out chunks of meat from different parts of the shoulder for that awesome mix of textures, pile everything into a bowl, and dole gravy all over it. Sometimes, they send it back and ask us to carve it up for them, but that's missing the point. Kinda like asking us to do them the favour of blowing out the candles on their birthday cake.

In Morocco, mechoui refers to a whole lamb roasted underground on a spit. Believe me, if I could dig a pit at Artichoke, I would. But we can't, so we take a lamb shoulder, rub it all over in mechoui spices, and roast it the entire day.

Meet Tim. He is the first and only fool who decided to take on the Lambgasm Challenge to finish one 2.5kg monster within 30 minutes. This is him before the challenge began. He was talking some shit about taking it down in 9 minutes or less.

The great thing about roasting a whole lamb shoulder on the bone is that it's so messy and inconsistent. This recipe calls for a 'square cut whole shoulder', which contains parts of the spine, neck, shoulder blade and ribs. With at least four muscle groups, this particular cut is a miracle of different textures, tastes and fat content. The bone adds insane flavour and renders delicious gravy, while the meat is softened throughout by the gelatinous connective tissue that melts during cooking.

> "In true sick bastard spirit, we still serve the lamb with a knife stuck straight in, like it was a beast we just hunted down."

Most good, Euro-centric butcheries in Singapore will be able to procure a lamb shoulder for you, but make sure to give them adequate time to prepare. You may substitute the shoulder with a bone-in lamb leg, which is smaller and easier to find. However, you will have to shorten the cooking time to ensure it doesn't end up dry and stringy.

SERVES 6-8

MECHOUI PASTE

2 tbsp mechoui spices (page 256)
2 tbsp apple cider vinegar
2 tbsp olive oil
1 tbsp sea salt

1 whole lamb shoulder, on the bone
   (about 2.4 to 2.8kg)
2 heads garlic
1 carrot, chopped
1 stick celery, chopped
2 white onions, chopped
2 bay leaves
1 handful fresh flat leaf parsley
   (Italian parsley)
2 sprigs thyme
1 cup white wine
4 tbsp smen (page 254)
Salt and pepper

Toum, to serve (page 253)
Smoked Tomato Ezme,
   to serve (page 257)
Artichoke-style Pickles,
   to serve (page 257)

THE LAMBGASM:
ARTICHOKE-STYLE SLOW-ROASTED LAMB SHOULDER

»»»»

To make the mechoui paste, mix the mechoui spices with the vinegar, olive oil and salt to form a paste.

Slash your lamb shoulder at small intervals of 3 to 4cm with the tip of a paring knife. Rub the mechoui paste all over the shoulder and into the scores. Leave to marinate for at least 4 hours or, ideally, overnight.

When ready to cook, preheat your oven to 240°C. Place all the ingredients into a deep roasting tray, with the lamb shoulder resting on the top. Roast for 15 minutes. Lower the temperature of the oven to 120°C and continue to cook for 5 to 6 hours, basting the shoulder with its own juices once or twice every hour. Your lamb shoulder is done when you twist one of the bones and it slips right out with almost no resistance—a sign that the meat is meltingly tender right through. Any resistance means the lamb is not ready yet; keep cooking. If halfway through the cooking time, you find that your meat is turning too dark in colour, cover it loosely with aluminum foil to prevent further browning.

Remove the lamb from the oven when it's done and allow it to rest in a warm place (or under aluminum foil) for at least 30 minutes. During this time, do not disturb the rest of the ingredients in the roasting tray. After 30 minutes, gently lift the lamb shoulder out of the roasting tray and onto a serving platter. Transfer the contents of the roasting tray into a saucepan and skim off any visible oil from the top. Bring the sauce to a rolling boil and reduce it by half. Season well with salt and pepper. Strain the gravy over the top of the lamb shoulder and present it to your guests along with generous bowls of toum, ezme and pickles. You don't even need to carve this with a knife; a pair of tongs is all you need to rip through the oh-so-tender meat.

... and this is Tim after the challenge.
He pussied out, as expected. The dude
couldn't stuff more lamb into himself.

CHAPTER 10

People of Artichoke, Past & Present

From top: Jia Zhen, from Overdoughs' creative team; Cong Wen, once a waiter, now a future rockstar chef.

》》》》》

When you spend 14 hours a day at work, you see more of your teammates than your family. They become your dysfunctional second family, one in which dry humping each other's legs is a daily affair and ball grabbing is a casual sport. The crew I have at Artichoke and Overdoughs means everything to me. Whenever a dish goes out, I make sure someone tastes it to make sure it's just right. If they say it's good to go, it is. I'd trust their judgements with my life.

Throughout the years, many great cooks have graced our kitchen with their presence. Whether interns, cooks or sous chefs, I encourage each of them to think freely, to take their creativity to the next level. I give them an idea to run with and mentor their development of the dish along the way.

Just a while ago, I set one of my chefs, Frankie, a project: to come up with a shawarma salad. Instead of serving it in a wrap—a typically solo affair—I wanted a more communal dish, pimped up with tons of sparkling greens and freshly prepared meats. None of that tired shredded iceberg lettuce shit, nawmeen? We talked about the vegetables: how about avocado for richness and texture, radicchio for a tinge of bitterness, and lots of fresh, pungent rocket for liveliness?

Hafiz and Addy, the supervisors

Shawn, the mezze guy

Joanna, hardworking intern

Mark, the GM and prank scapegoat

Then the meat: instead of mystery meat rotated for hours on a dry spit, what about using beef short ribs? Brisket? Shredded or sliced? Braised, roasted or grilled? Finally we needed a sauce to string the elements together elegantly, while still evoking messy shawarma wraps eaten on drunken late nights by the curb. With all that roiling around in Frankie's head, I sent him home to piece all the elements together.

Back at work, he prepared variations of this salad. We sat down, analysed each version, talked through what we liked or didn't like

Melissa, garde manger chef

about it. The final recipe was a winner of avocado, red cabbage, roasted onions and rocket, topped with juicy slices of wet-roasted beef short rib rubbed with shawarma spices. We settled upon a truffled tahini dressing—elevated, yet true to its roots. And we served it proudly on our dinner menu.

All of us find this process particularly fulfilling. It sure beats the crap out of cooking the same thing, day in and day out, like a damn robot. This chapter is dedicated to the bright fellas who've made their mark at Artichoke.

Ron, one of my sous chefs.

ROASTED PUMPKIN

½ large pumpkin, chopped
   into large chunks
1 red onion, quartered
2 tsp clear honey
2 tbsp red wine vinegar
2 sprigs thyme
4 tbsp olive oil
Salt and pepper

MARMITE HONEY DRESSING

1 tbsp Marmite
2 tbsp hot water
2 tbsp clear honey
2 tbsp lemon juice
1 clove garlic, finely chopped
½ handful fresh coriander,
   finely chopped
4 tbsp extra virgin olive oil
Salt and pepper

PUMPKIN SEED DUKKA

2 tbsp pumpkin seeds,
   toasted (page 19)
1 tbsp white sesame seeds, toasted
1 tsp cumin seeds, toasted
1 tsp coriander seeds, toasted
1 tsp sumac (page 17)
1 tsp sea salt

1 handful fresh mint, roughly torn
½ cup crumbled feta cheese

ROASTED PUMPKIN WITH MARMITE HONEY,

PUMPKIN SEED DUKKA AND FETA

In recent years, zichar (Singaporean 'home style' food) stalls have been quietly progressing Singaporean cuisine by adding subtle new touches to familiar dishes. Pork ribs are coated in a coffee sauce; salted egg yolk is now a ubiquitous coating on selected crustaceans; Marmite can be found glazing chicken and pork. In a bid to acknowledge the growing clout of Marmite in local cuisine, I threw the challenge of using it in a dish to Melissa. She was an intern from the Culinary Institute of America (Singapore), and is now a full-time staffer. The combination of pumpkin, feta and fresh greens wasn't a new one, but she blew my mind with the Marmite honey—sweet, not overpowering, and packed with a killer umami boost. This salad goes great with roast red meats, like lamb or beef.

》》》》》

To make the roasted pumpkin, first preheat your oven to 190°C. Toss the pumpkin and onion wedges with the other ingredients and season well with salt and pepper. Roast the pumpkin for 40 minutes, taking care not to let the vegetables burn. If they start to brown too quickly within the suggested time, reduce the oven temperature slightly.

Meanwhile, make the honey dressing by whisking the Marmite with the hot water to loosen it up. Add the remaining ingredients and whisk briskly again. Add salt and pepper to taste.

To make the pumpkin seed dukka, coarsely crush each of the seeds separately with a pestle and mortar. Mix them in a bowl with the sumac and sea salt.

To serve, place the pumpkin and onions on a serving platter, drizzle with the dressing and scatter generously with the pumpkin seed dukka, mint and feta. This dish is best served at room temperature.

SERVES
4*

BASTURMA AND MINTED PEA FLATBREADS

WITH LABNEH

MINTED PEA SALAD

½ cup frozen baby peas,
thawed and drained

½ shallot, thinly sliced

½ clove garlic, finely chopped

½ handful fresh mint, finely chopped

½ stalk spring onion, finely chopped

1 tsp finely grated lemon zest

1 tbsp lemon juice

4 tbsp extra virgin olive oil

Pinch of freshly ground black pepper

Sea salt

2 flatbreads
(preferably pita breads, page 18)

1 clove garlic, split in half

2 tbsp labneh (page 260)

8 to 10 thin slices basturma
(or other seasoned, cured beef
such as cecina or bresaola)

* Makes 2 flatbreads

Diagram 1.0

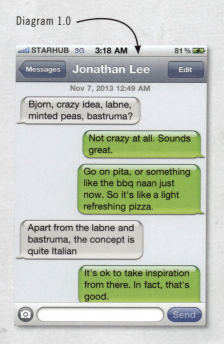

Jonathan, my sous chef, has been with me since day one. He was on my opening team as a line cook, and has more or less absorbed everything there is to know about Artichoke and its food. The guy's extremely creative, often sending me random texts at random hours for dish ideas (see diagram 1.0). This dish was a hit on our menu when it rolled out.

»»»»

To make the minted pea salad, mix all the ingredients in a bowl and season well. Set aside for at least 1 hour to allow the flavours to mingle.

In a dry pan, toast the flatbreads over high heat till they are slightly charred and crispy. While they are still hot, rub them with the cut sides of the garlic, just as if you are making garlic bread. Spread the labneh over each flatbread, and top with the minted pea salad. Divide the slices of basturma across each flatbread. Quarter each flatbread and serve.

Coke + Red Wine
$5.5
& el Bulli dudes
750ml bottle
ichoke
cafe+bar
SOME

EAT
COMMUNALLY

2 to 3 large chicken thigh fillets,
   skin left on
2 tbsp mechoui spices (page 256)
2 tbsp apple cider vinegar
Zest of ½ a lemon
4 tbsp olive oil
Vegetable oil, for frying
Salt and pepper

2 cups hummus (page 254)
2 tbsp pine nuts, toasted (page 19)
1 tbsp pomegranate arils
⅛ red onion, very finely sliced
1 small handful herbs
   (such as mint, coriander,
   parsley, etc.), roughly torn
Pomegranate molasses,
   to garnish (optional)
Extra virgin olive oil, for drizzling
Lemon wedges, to serve
Flatbread, to serve (page 18)

CRISPY CHICKEN OVER HUMMUS

We never actually served this dish at Artichoke; it was more a staff experiment that went crazy well. During a staff outing at another Middle Eastern restaurant, we stumbled upon a simple chicken shawarma served over hummus that blew our collective mind. Shavings of chicken, slightly crispy around the edges, were thrown over hummus and drowned in standard-issue Maggi chicken gravy. In our version, we wanted to highlight the crispy bits so we worked on getting all of the skin nice and crisp, not just the edges. Never too much of a good thing, I say.

»»»»

In a large bowl, rub the fillets thoroughly with the mechoui spices, vinegar, lemon zest and olive oil. Let marinate for at least 4 hours, or better yet, overnight.

Place a heavy-based frying pan over medium heat. Drizzle in enough vegetable oil to coat the pan. Season the chicken generously on both sides with salt and pepper, then lay them, skin side down, in the hot oil. Turn the heat to medium-low and allow the chicken to cook undisturbed for about 5 minutes, or until the chicken is cooked through. What you are trying to achieve is an extremely crispy, well-browned skin; the low-medium heat ensures that the spices don't burn in the meantime. Flip over a piece of chicken and tap the skin with your tongs. If it feels and sounds super crispy, flip all the pieces over and cook the other sides for 2 minutes more. If the skin is not totally crispy yet, flip it back over and keep cooking till it is. Once the chicken is done, remove from the pan, and place crispy-side up in a warm place to rest for 5 minutes. Do not cover the chicken with foil or anything else that would trap steam and ruin the crisp skin.

To serve, spoon the hummus over a large communal platter. Slice the chicken into Kit Kat-sized fingers. Place the fingers skin-side up over the hummus and garnish with a scattering of the pine nuts, pomegranate arils, onion slices and herbs. Drizzle with some pomegranate molasses and extra virgin olive oil. Serve with lemon wedges and flatbread. Get stuck in.

It's like a whole friggin' cow just exploded over a bowl of chickpea soup. Enjoy.

This is Haziz, my ex-deputy at Artichoke and the harira's architect.

The poster I brainstormed for this dish. Inspiration: the ramen champions of yore.

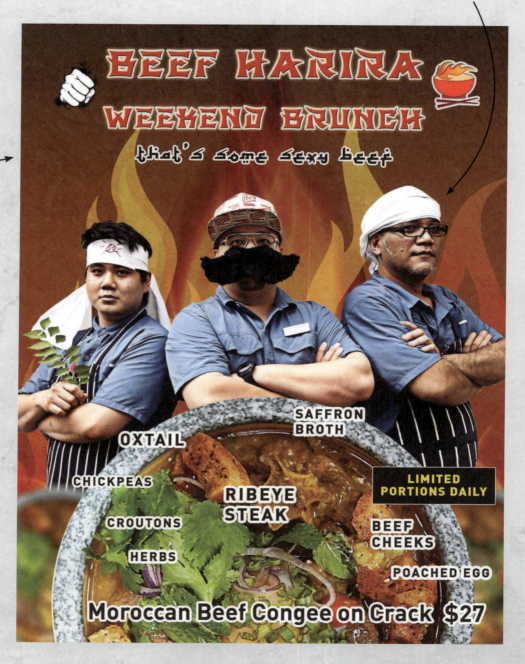

HARIRA SPICE BASE

1 large red onion, chopped
4 cloves garlic, chopped
2 handfuls fresh coriander
  (leaves and stalks included)
1 tbsp turmeric powder
1 tbsp ginger powder
1 tbsp black pepper
1 tbsp hot paprika
1 tsp cinnamon powder
1 tsp chilli powder
Pinch of saffron strands

6 tbsp vegetable oil
2 large tomatoes, chopped
4 shallots, chopped
600 g beef brisket and/or beef cheeks
800 g oxtail
2 litres water,
  plus additional for adjusting
Salt and pepper
1 cup canned chickpeas,
  washed and drained
2 tbsp smen (page 254), optional
2 cups long grain rice, cooked
4 eggs

2 handfuls fresh herbs
  (mint, parsley, coriander, etc.)
Toasted croutons, to serve (optional)
Lemon wedges, to serve

HAZIZ'S SUPER PIMPED-UP
HARIRA

The Artichoke-style harira was dreamed up by Haziz, my previous sous chef, and me. Haziz is a big meat-and-potatoes guy and a damn wizard at building flavour in soups and stews. We wanted to turn harira from a humble peasant's stew into something punchy and thick and rich, a meal in itself. In the Maghreb, the dish is a tomato-based soup enhanced by scraps of meat, lentils and rice. Our version would be over the top; no skimping on the meat here. Haziz, taking inspiration from Vietnamese pho, put together a variety of cuts: oxtail, ribeye steak and beef cheeks. Then we jacked up the carb content to make the dish even more substantial. It's like a whole friggin' cow just exploded over a bowl of chickpea soup. Enjoy.

»»»»

To make the spice base, blend all the ingredients in a food processor into a coarse paste.

In a heavy-based stockpot, heat up the vegetable oil over medium heat and cook the paste for 5 minutes, stirring continuously. Add in the tomatoes, shallots, beef brisket, oxtail and water. Add more water if necessary to just cover the meat. Bring to a simmer and cook for 4 hours over low heat, constantly skimming away any oil that rises to the top. As the harira cooks, continue adding water when necessary to keep the level of the soup high enough to cover the meat. After 4 hours, the meat should fall apart to the touch. Remove the beef and chop it into 2cm cubes. Return these chunks to the broth. Season well with salt and pepper. You can put the entire stockpot of harira away at this time until you and your gang are ready to eat.

When you're finally ready, bring the broth back to a simmer. Add in the chickpeas and cook for 10 minutes more. Add in the smen and the cooked rice and turn the heat to high. Bring to a boil. Crack the eggs into the boiling broth, leaving some space between each egg and turn off the heat immediately.

Bring the whole pot to the table and top with the herbs. By this time, the heat in the broth should have lightly poached the eggs. Divide the harira among four bowls, making sure each bowl gets some oxtail, beef brisket and/or cheek, chickpeas, rice, a softly poached egg, and a good amount of hot, beefy broth. Pass around some croutons and lemon wedges. Slurp noisily.

KATAIFI ALMOND CRUNCH

¼ standard packet
  or 100 g kataifi pastry
1 cup unsalted butter, melted
½ cup almond flakes,
  toasted (page 19)
½ cup clear honey

APPLE FILLING

½ cup unsalted butter
8 Granny Smith apples,
  peeled and chopped
¼ cup raisins or sultanas
½ cup brown sugar
1 tbsp cinnamon powder
Zest of ½ a lemon

1 pinch dried rose petals (optional)
4 generous scoops vanilla
  or honey gelato

TURKISH CHEATERBUG APPLE CRUMBLE

WITH KATAIFI ALMOND CRUNCH

I set Melissa another project: to make a Middle Eastern crumble-style dessert. No traditional English crumble pastry allowed. She turned to kataifi, a Levantine shredded filo pastry. Cutting it up into short strips yielded a sort of crispy mix, perfect for sprinkling atop warm apple filling. We call this a 'cheaterbug' crumble because the elements can be prepped beforehand and assembled quickly at the last minute. Kataifi pastry can be bought in raw form from supermarkets.

»»»»

To make the kataifi almond crunch, cut the kataifi pastry into short lengths of 1 to 2cm. Toss with the butter to coat all the strands. It should be glossy and look like fried rice vermicelli from a Chinese takeaway. Preheat your oven to 180°C. Spread the buttered pastry over a baking sheet and bake for 20 minutes, or until the strands turn golden-brown and crispy. Remove from the oven and, while still hot, fold in the almond flakes and honey. Allow to cool.

To make the apple filling, heat up the butter in a frying pan over high heat till it melts. Sauté the apple chunks and raisins in the butter for 2 minutes. Add in the brown sugar, cinnamon powder and lemon zest and cook for 5 minutes more, or until the apples have softened and the sugar has formed a glossy caramel.

To serve, place the apple filling in a large casserole, or four individual ones. Warm the casserole in a hot oven for several minutes, then top with a 1cm layer of kataifi almond crunch. Scatter some dried rose petals over and pop on a scoop of gelato for each person.

Tattoos & Tomatoes

CHAPTER 11

>>>>>>

If there's one thing I'm opinionated about, it's eating local. Though we do import ingredients at Artichoke and Overdoughs, we try our best to use local alternatives on the menu. As of now, at least 30 per cent of our dinner menu is committed to dishes that showcase fantastic Singapore-grown mushrooms, tomatoes, Asian kale, black fungus, eggs and more.

We want to show fellow Singaporeans that what we've got growing on home soil is pretty damn tasty too. What's more, the benefits are manifold: produce is undeniably fresher; we're supporting small, non-industrial Singaporean farmers; our carbon footprint is significantly lowered.

Allow me to clarify: I am not against imported goods. Come on, I know too that without flying produce in, we'd never be able to slurp up uni pasta or get wasted off absinthe here, and the only meat we'll ever eat would be quail and frog from local farms. I drive a delivery van myself, so I'm also guilty of pumping nasty gases into the air.

I know that locavorism isn't a one-stop solution for the world's dire food issues. In some cases, importing produce might even be the lesser evil—rod-and-line-caught yellowfin tuna from North America, despite racking up higher transport emissions, is considerably better than tuna trawled indiscriminately from closer waters.

But I believe locavorism is an essential aspect of eating sustainably. Sometimes we refrain from including Jerusalem artichokes and Tuscan black cabbages in our dishes—even though

We want to show fellow Singaporeans that what we've got growing on home soil is pretty damn tasty too.

BJORN
SHEN

BJORN
LOW

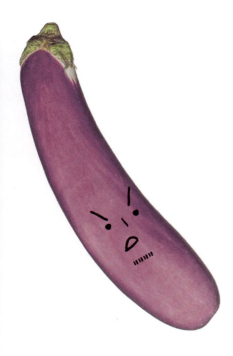

we'd really like to—just because of the distance they're sourced from. You can't brag about 'sustainable' baby carrots, plucked out of the ground with oh-so-little-impact, when you then proceed to fly them halfway across the globe twice a week. For some restaurants, bandying about the S word is another way of bragging that their ingredients are fancy and imported. It's a PR smokescreen, with no genuine interest in environmentalism.

Back in 2012, my brother-in-law Ryan set up a meeting between me and his friend who'd just returned from the UK. Apparently, this guy's name was Bjorn as well, and he had just started up an urban farming initiative. We clicked immediately. He was a real unpretentious guy and a modern day hippie who'd spent the previous year herding sheep and engaging in 'biodynamic farming' (whatever that is) in the British countryside, with no running water and electricity. He returned to Singapore to spearhead the urban farming movement with his new company, The Edible Garden City Project (now called Edible Gardens). Along with **co-founder Rob Pearce**, they worked towards their dream of converting public spaces and rooftops in the city into lush gardens brimming with edible produce. Bjorn Low wanted to change the way Singaporeans looked at food, farming and sustainability. He was totally ahead of the curve, and way in over his head. He was—and is—a total idealist. But despite his big ideas, he never put on airs of self-importance, choosing **instead to espouse his values through actions and his tattoos**. (Bjorn's legs are inked with trees, tomatoes, leaves—the guy really loves Momma Nature.) His gumption has yielded results. Today, the Edible Gardens team are rock stars in their own right, with two rooftop farms, multiple community-driven veggie gardens and a happy abundance of projects.

As for me, I believe in practising what I preach. Throughout all this, Artichoke and Edible Gardens have been working hand in hand. Their crew continues to manage and maintain the restaurant's 300sq ft garden. Our stacked crates are teeming with all manner of mint, borage, basil, tomatoes, baby eggplants and more, which we use in relishes and condiments. They put us in touch with anyone new who grows local produce. It's all ridiculously symbiotic. Bjorn and I have collaborated on dining events, given Earth Day speeches on sourcing locally and urban farming, and contributed to countless media interviews.

It ain't easy being green, a famous frog once said. But it sure as hell is a whole lot of fun.

Calabrian chilli

Indian borage

Various types of mint

3 to 4 tbsp smen (page 254)

2 cloves garlic, thinly sliced

1 shallot, thinly sliced

400 g assorted mushrooms, coarsely chopped

1 tsp baharat (page 255, optional)

2 sprigs thyme

Salt and pepper

1 tbsp lemon juice

MUSHROOMS FRIED IN SMEN

Some of my favourite mushroom varieties—locally grown, of course—are abalone, willow, golden cup and yellow oyster. These are essentially Asian mushrooms which add a distinctly Asian profile to a dish. I figured since we're cooking in Singapore, why not use produce from our own backyard? The addition of smen (Moroccan preserved butter) adds just a light Middle Eastern touch. For a winning brekkie, serve these mushrooms with scrambled eggs (page 194) and toast.

»»»»

Heat a non-stick frying pan over medium heat. When the pan is hot, add the smen, reserving 1 tablespoon to pop in at the very end of cooking. Immediately add the garlic and shallots, and fry for half a minute. Add the mushrooms to the pan along with the baharat and thyme. Toss to coat the mushrooms with the smen. Cook for 3 to 4 minutes, tossing occasionally, until the mushrooms start to soften. Season well with salt and pepper, and add the lemon juice and final tablespoon of smen. Toss once more.

Some of my favourite mushroom varieties are abalone, willow, golden cup and yellow oyster.

EAT
LOCALLY

VINAIGRETTE

1 tsp smoked paprika
½ tsp cumin powder
4 tbsp sherry vinegar
½ tsp honey
8 tbsp extra virgin olive oil
1 clove garlic, finely chopped
1 shallot, finely chopped
1 small handful fresh mint leaves,
    roughly torn
Salt and pepper

CRISPY VINE LEAVES

1 jar vine leaves in brine (you only
    need 4 leaves from the jar)
Vegetable oil, for frying

1 punnet, or 250 g cherry tomatoes
1 block haloumi, soaked and sliced into
    1.5cm-thick slabs (page 16)
1 tbsp olive oil
Clear honey, for drizzling

GRILLED HALOUMI
WITH MOORISH TOMATO SALAD AND CRISPY VINE LEAVES

A perennial favourite at the restaurant, this combination of salty, squeaky cheese and sweet, juicy tomatoes is known to create sensory overload on people's taste buds. The addition of fried vine leaves brings a crispy texture to the dish and bumps it up a notch. The tomatoes usually come from Artichoke's garden plot, but on days when yield is low (bugs and bad weather are our greatest enemies), we bulk up supply with orders from a local farm.

»»»»

To make the vinaigrette, mix all the ingredients in a bowl and whisk to combine. Adjust with more vinegar, honey or oil to taste. Season to taste with salt and pepper.

To make the crispy vine leaves, remove the vine leaves from the jar and rinse well to remove any excess brine. Pat dry with kitchen paper. Heat some oil in a shallow frying pan over medium heat. Add the leaves and fry on both sides till crisp.

To make the tomato salad, carve a small, shallow 'X' on the base of each cherry tomato with the tip of a small knife. Throw the tomatoes into a pot of boiling water. After 30 seconds, drain the tomatoes and put them into a bowl of water and ice. Upon cooling, the skins of the tomatoes should be loose enough to slide off. Peel all the tomatoes. Toss the tomatoes in the vinaigrette and leave to marinate for at least 30 minutes.

To finish the dish, pat dry the slices of haloumi. Heat the olive oil over medium heat in a non-stick frying pan. Add the slabs of haloumi and fry for 1 to 2 minutes on each side till golden-brown. Place the haloumi slices on a plate and spoon the tomatoes over. Top with the crispy vine leaves and drizzle the dish with the honey. Eat this while hot to avoid the cheese going rubbery when it cools down.

TZATZIKI OF LOCAL GREENS
WITH ROASTED SESAME SEEDS

500 g locally sourced leafy greens,
   washed and chopped
3 tbsp olive oil
5 cloves garlic, finely chopped
Salt and pepper
1 stalk spring onion, finely chopped
½ handful fresh dill, finely chopped
500 g thick Greek yoghurt
1 tbsp lemon juice
1 tbsp white sesame seeds,
   toasted (page 19)
Extra virgin olive oil, for drizzling

*Makes 4 cups

Of course, non-locally sourced greens will work with this recipe. We're not veggie Nazis. Try it with anything leafy, such as spinach, kale and chard.

I was once brought to an organic farm which specialises in just four greens: xiao bai cai, kai lan, kang kong and chye sim. Eating the vegetables was a revelation—they somehow tasted, for lack of a better word, pure. More like themselves than other varieties. I didn't want to mess too much with them, so I just cooked them with tons of garlic, Chinese-style, before folding them into yoghurt to make an Artichoke-style tzatziki. The dish is best eaten cold, as a dip for bread, or as a refreshing condiment to accompany grilled fish or meat.

〉〉〉〉〉

Pat dry the local greens. Heat the olive oil in a wok over high heat and fry the garlic till fragrant. Add the greens and cook for 3 minutes, or until they are well wilted. Season to taste with salt and pepper. Transfer the greens to a colander and squeeze out as much excess water as possible. Allow to cool in the fridge.

When the cooked greens are cool, place them in a large mixing bowl and mix in the spring onions, dill, yoghurt and lemon juice. Season to taste again with salt and pepper.

To serve, dollop a large spoonful of the tzatziki onto a plate and spread it out with the back of a spoon. Sprinkle generously with the sesame seeds and drizzle with the extra virgin olive oil.

2 tbsp unsalted butter

2 tbsp garlic, finely chopped

2 tbsp shallots, finely chopped

100 g spinach, washed and roughly chopped (preferably locally grown)

100 g mushrooms, cleaned and roughly chopped (preferably locally grown, page 143)

Salt and pepper

½ cup chicken or vegetable stock

½ cup heavy cream, plus additional for adjusting

200 g bee tai mak (silver needle noodles)

¾ cup shredded cheese mix (we use equal parts mozzarella, string cheese and kashkaval, but you could use other cheeses like cheddar, gruyere, feta, etc.)

1 tsp chopped dill

1 tbsp breadcrumbs, toasted

SINGAPORE 'MAK & CHEESE'

I was inspired very much by a chef named May Chow who owns and runs Little Bao, a killer little place in Hong Kong that slings out Asian versions of hamburgers. Think steamed buns filled with fish tempura, lemongrass fennel salad and a tamarind palm sugar glaze. Anyway, she's got a special kind of magic with Asian ingredients, and one of her stellar side dishes is a HK Mac & Cheese made with cheung fun (rolled rice noodles) smothered in mentaiko and cheese, and baked till bubbly and crusty. I was so bowled over by the idea that I worked on cooking up a Singaporean equivalent once I got back. I eventually settled on putting together my childhood go-to noodles, bee tai mak (aka mouse tail or silver needle noodles), with mushrooms and spinach from the Kranji Countryside farms. This is one of the greatest pleasures of my job—taking inspiration from other great chefs.

〉〉〉〉〉

In a heavy-based saucepan, heat the butter over medium-high heat. Add in the garlic and shallots and fry for 1 to 2 minutes, till they turn translucent. Add in the spinach and mushrooms, and cook for 4 minutes more till the spinach wilts. Season well with salt and pepper. Tip the spinach and mushroom mixture into a colander and allow any excess juice from the vegetables to drain off. Press on the vegetable mixture with a spoon to force out even more juice. You want to end up with a relatively dry vegetable mixture that isn't going to water down your cheese sauce.

In a separate heavy-based saucepan (or in the same one that you wash out), bring the stock and cream to a boil. Add the noodles into the boiling liquid, along with the cooked vegetable mixture. Bring the mixture to a simmer and cook for 1 to 2 minutes more, allowing the noodles to soften and the sauce to thicken. Add more cream if necessary to keep the mixture from being too dry. Remove from the heat, stir in the cheese and mix till well combined. Season again if necessary, being mindful that the cheese you've just added in could already be quite salty.

Plate up the 'Mak & Cheese' in a shallow bowl, then sprinkle with the dill and breadcrumbs.

CHAPTER 12

Staff Meals

>>>>>

In Copenhagen, I had the pleasure of spending half a day with Michelin-starred chef Henrik Yde-Andersen at his Modern Thai restaurant, Kiin Kiin. When it was about time for the staff meal, I saw one of his sous chefs working furiously in the kitchen, churning out dish after dish. Dinner service was still a while away. I asked why he was prepping so early.

"No, that's for the staff meal," Henrik looked me dead in the eye. "We're fully booked later, but the most important people we need to feed tonight are our staff." That sentence blew me away. As did the meal that followed. Seared beef salad and pork collar stir-fried with long beans were served atop a steaming mound of white rice. We then poured a rich pork rib broth over everything, crowned

Our weekly family feast is also actually quite fuckin' epic.

it with an umami bomb of fermented shrimp relish, and dug in. We ate from mixing bowls. It was easily the best food I had in the city.

Back at Artichoke, after brunch service every Sunday, we reach into the depths of our fridges, pull out the week's leftovers and cook up a mongrel meal for staff lunch. Since Sunday brunch is the last service day of the week, we're stuck with odd bits of really good produce that surely won't last till we reopen the following Tuesday. All these little morsels added together can amount to a whole lot of food. So what do we do with all these ingredients?

Anything we damn well want.

Before you start imagining a bunch of brutes squatting out back eating some gnarly sludge out of mixing bowls, let me tell you that our weekly family feast is also actually quite fuckin' epic: there are huge-ass tiger prawns, inch-thick bacon steaks, lamb sausage and ketchup fried rice, smoked salmon on honeyed pancakes with Jim Beam sour cream, chicken skin donuts and other such dubious delights.

Many instances of 'culinary genius' have occurred by thoughtlessly chucking a bunch of leftovers together and sticking them in the oven or fryer. The more Frankenstein-esque the ingredient combinations, the better. Most times, we reap what we sow. Ribeye steak braised in Ribena tastes just like… ribeye steak and Ribena. It's pretty nasty. But every once in a blue moon, by some sheer stroke of dumb luck, one of these creations actually tastes good enough to make our taste buds scream in ecstasy. Sometimes, they're so good that we attempt to retrace our steps, recall what the hell we just did, and then refine them to a point where they're 'gourmet' enough to put on our menu and have people order them. I love my job.

Anyway, here are some awesome dishes that came about during staff meal 'accidents'. I'm pretty sure that such silly happenings occur in the kitchens of other great restaurants too, but I reckon we're the only ones dumb enough to make this kind of information public. Good PR and overall common sense dictate that when faced with flukey success of this nature, one should instead opt for the "Oh we spent 2 months developing this recipe with our pastry team" spiel. Well, balls to that, we say. Here's the truth.

Facing page: A brunch staff meal. What you see is half of it. This page, from top: Shakshouka with two whole fish thrown in; another shakshouka garnished with a single slice of haloumi.

EAT
LIKE AN
ANIMAL

BASE INGREDIENTS

8 hash browns, deep-fried
12 Butter-whipped Scrambled Eggs
(page 194)
1 cup grated cheese (such as
cheddar, Monterey Jack,
Gouda, Emmental, etc.)

EXTRA INGREDIENTS
—TAKE YOUR PICK, OR PICK ALL

Bacon strips, fried till crispy
Thick-cut ham chunks
Sausages, grilled and
chopped into chunks
Beef strips, grilled
Assorted mushrooms,
sautéed (page 143)
Spinach, sautéed
Cherry tomatoes, roasted
Croissants, torn into chunks

Maple syrup, to serve
Sriracha sauce, to serve

> Though you can pick
> what you want to add, the
> scrambled eggs and cheese
> are essential. They act as
> binders to draw the entire
> dish together.

BREAKFAST SMASH-UP

This is less a recipe than a gentle guiding hand to making your own smash-up. It came about once after brunch service, when the guys and I were scrubbing down in the kitchen. Though we were hungry, we didn't want to stop working. So we smashed up some fry-up leftovers lying around, divided it into mixing bowls, and ate it with a spoon while cleaning. Efficient, no? Before you start crying "gross!", just know that all we want is for the flavours of the ingredients to meld together, instead of having them kept separate (as we usually do when we eat them politely off a plate).

»»»»

Start by placing the hash browns, scrambled eggs and cheese into a large mixing bowl. Add anything else you fancy from the 'Extra Ingredients' list. Grab a potato masher and start crushing everything lightly. The hash browns and eggs should start to break up and mix with the rest of the ingredients, and the now-melted cheese should act as a bit of a binder. Observe the magic in front of you: mushrooms bleeding their juices into the eggs; hash browns softening in the grease from the bacon and/or sausages; cheese going melty-stringy and winding itself over morsels of ham. Remember, we're not trying to turn this into dog food; we're just trying to squish a little essence out of each ingredient and allow them to get jiggy with each other in the bowl. So avoid the urge to overdo it on the crushing part, despite how fun it may seem.

Squirt on some maple syrup and sriracha to serve.

GINGER ALE PORK CHOPS

MARINADE

1 can ginger ale

2 tbsp Dijon mustard

2 cloves garlic, finely chopped

2 shallots, finely chopped

1 salted anchovy fillet, chopped

1 handful fresh sage, chopped

½ tsp fennel seeds,
   toasted and crushed (page 19)

4 large, bone-in pork chops

Olive oil, for frying

Salt and pepper

My pal Ben used to work here as a dishwasher. His favourite drink was ginger ale, so one day we decided to dedicate a dish to him. Coca-Cola braised chicken and root beer ribs have been done before; why not ginger ale-marinated pork chops? (Especially since ginger and pork are a common pairing.) The acid in the soft drink tenderizes the pork well, and the sugars yield a nice caramelly sweetness upon cooking. Remember to use bone-in pork chops for the most flavourful results. Rocket and Sweet Corn Tabbouleh (page 39) goes great with this dish.

»»»»

To make the marinade, mix all the marinade ingredients together.

Pour the marinade over the pork chops and massage it lightly into the meat. Place in a sealed container and leave to marinate for at least 4 hours in the fridge.

Take the pork out of the fridge 30 minutes before you start cooking and allow the chops to warm to room temperature. Heat up a non-stick frying pan over medium heat and brush off as much solid material from the pork chops as you can; these bits are a pain in the butt and will only burn while the chops cook. Add a little olive oil to the pan, and cook the chops for 3 to 4 minutes on each side. Season each side generously with salt and pepper while cooking. Remove the chops from the pan and allow them to rest in a warm place.

Return the pan to the heat and pour in the marinade. Allow to simmer and thicken to a gravy-like consistency. Season the sauce to taste with salt and pepper and pour it over the warm pork chops to serve.

Coca-Cola braised chicken and root beer ribs have been done before; why not ginger ale-marinated pork chops?

GINGER MANDARIN SYRUP

4 mandarin oranges, peeled and
　separated into segments
1 thumb-sized piece fresh ginger
2 tbsp lemon juice
1 handful fresh mint leaves
1 stick cinnamon
2 star anises
8 tbsp caster sugar
1 cup water

Ice cubes, to serve
2 cans ginger ale
Mandarin orange segments,
　to garnish
Lemon wedges, to garnish
Mint leaves, to garnish

CHINESE NEW YEAR
GINGER BEER

Each Chinese New Year, our suppliers send us truckloads of hampers and produce. Once, we had four cartons of mandarin oranges just sitting around the restaurant, starting to get a little stanky. To make good use of them, I juiced all of them during the staff party to make a mocktail. To reference the festival, I wanted to spice things up a little—literally. I threw in typically Chinese, five-spice powder elements: cinnamon, star anise, ginger, etc. Voila—a quick, refreshing CNY-ready drink.

》》》》》

To make the syrup, place all the ingredients except for the water into a saucepan and bash everything up with the bottom of a ladle, as if you were muddling a very large cocktail. Add the water and bring to a boil. Allow to boil for 5 minutes and then leave to cool. Strain out the solids.

To finish the drink, place some ice into four cups and pour in 3 parts ginger ale to 1 part ginger mandarin syrup. Garnish with mandarin segments, lemon wedges and mint leaves.

BASTURMA-STYLE CURED TUNA

½ cup sea salt or kosher salt
½ cup soft brown sugar
2 sprigs thyme
1 clove garlic, finely chopped
1 sashimi-grade tuna loin (about 200 g)

BASTURMA SPICE MIX

¼ cup hot or sweet paprika
¼ cup ground fenugreek
1 tbsp cinnamon powder
1 tbsp coarsely ground black pepper
1 tsp ground cumin
½ tsp chilli powder

2 small shallots, thinly sliced into rings
1 tbsp lemon juice
1 cup pomelo sacs
½ stalk spring onion, finely chopped
½ green chilli, thinly sliced
4 tbsp extra virgin olive oil
Salt
Japanese mayonnaise, as topping
    (Kewpie brand, optional)
1 tbsp white sesame seeds,
    toasted (page 19)

BASTURMA-STYLE TUNA
WITH POMELO, ONIONS AND ROASTED SESAME

We created this dish during Chinese New Year 2012, to pay homage to the ubiquitous festive dish, yusheng (raw fish served with shredded vegetables and a variety of toppings). Instead of using raw salmon, we cured a tuna loin in salt, sugar and basturma spices. Unlike the traditional basturma-cured beef, which is dried for months to yield a dry, prosciutto-like product, we went for a quicker gravlax-like cure. The addition of pomelo and sesame seeds was the final nod to the Chinese original.

>>>>>

To cure the tuna, combine the salt, sugar, thyme and garlic in a bowl and mix well. Rub this mixture thoroughly onto the surface of the tuna. Chill the tuna in the fridge for 5 to 6 hours, then rinse off the curing mix and pat dry with kitchen paper.

To make the spice mix, combine the ingredients and rub onto the cured tuna. Return to the fridge for at least 1 hour, or until ready to serve.

Mix the shallots with the lemon juice and allow to pickle for at least 5 minutes. Place the pomelo, spring onion, chilli and extra virgin olive oil into a mixing bowl, then add the pickled shallots along with its pickling juices. Toss to combine, and season to taste with salt. Slice the tuna thinly crosswise along the loin and lay flat on a plate. Place a small dollop of mayonnaise on each slice of tuna, then top with the pomelo salad and a little of its dressing. Finish up with a sprinkle of the sesame seeds.

Bacon is Evil, We Must Destroy It with Our Teeth

CHAPTER

13

》》》》》

Prudence isn't really one of my strong suits, which is why I'm now divulging the top-secret skeleton method behind how we, at Artichoke, conceptualise each new dish. The ritual is simple:

Step #1: Deep-fry the main ingredient. If it doesn't work, we go on to

Step #2: Drench the mofo in mayo and/or cheese. If that doesn't fly either, there's

Step #3: Pairing it with bacon.

Ah, bacon. I have an unhealthy obsession with the streaks of fat and unbearable saltiness; it all makes my world go round. Waxing lyrical about something so close to my heart is impossible, so I'll leave you with pictorial proof that this fetish for the candy of the porcine world runs deep, deep in my genetic makeup:

DAD

BOURBON BUTTER

1 shot glass worth of bourbon
   (such as Wild Turkey, Jim Beam, etc.)
150 g salted butter,
   at room temperature

BACON SWEET POTATO HASH

500 g slab belly bacon,
   coarsely chopped into 3cm cubes
2 large sweet potatoes,
   peeled and coarsely chopped
1 large red onion,
   peeled and coarsely chopped
1 head garlic, separated into cloves
3 sprigs thyme
3 sprigs rosemary
2 tbsp unsalted butter,
   at room temperature
Salt and pepper

Vegetable oil, for frying
8 eggs
Maple syrup, for drizzling
Salad leaves and dressing of your
   choice, to serve (totally optional)
4 thick slices of bread (preferably
   sourdough or ciabatta), toasted

BACON SWEET POTATO HASH
WITH FRIED EGGS AND BOURBON BUTTER

A CHALLENGE BJORN DISH

The first dish to emerge from the 'Challenge Bjorn', well, challenge. We didn't want to overdo it on the crazy and started at first gear. We picked ingredients that complement each other: bacon, sweet potato and, of course, bourbon. Be sure to use thick-cut belly bacon, not that skinny streaky stuff. If you can eat bacon thick, I say, eat it thick. Belly bacon can be found at any good supermarket or butcher; alternatively you may use speck.

»»»»»

To make the bourbon butter, whisk the bourbon with the butter till well combined. If you want to get a little fancy, you can roll it up into a log with cling film. Alternatively, just transfer it into another bowl and refrigerate till firm.

To make the hash, preheat your oven to 160°C. Mix all the ingredients in a roasting tray, ensuring that everything is coated in butter. Roast uncovered for 30 to 45 minutes, until the ingredients are browned and the vegetables are soft. Toss the ingredients every 15 minutes to ensure everything browns evenly. Remove from the oven and season to taste with salt and pepper.

Fry the eggs sunny-side up in sets of 2. Heat up the vegetable oil over high heat in a non-stick frying pan. Crack 2 eggs in and cook till the whites get crispy around the edges but the yolk is still runny. Remove and repeat with the other eggs. Add more oil along the way if necessary.

Divide the hash across four plates and top each with a pair of fried eggs. Drizzle maple syrup over the eggs and garnish with some salad and dressing, if using. Serve with a knob of bourbon butter and hot toast.

ROCK OUT
WITH YOUR
PORK OUT

400 g slab belly bacon,
   chopped into 2cm cubes
½ large red onion, thickly sliced

SHAKIN' MIX
1 tbsp fish sauce
1 tbsp sugar
1 handful fresh coriander leaves
1 handful fresh mint leaves
4 tbsp roasted peanuts (you may use
   the common store-bought variety)
½ cup cherry tomatoes, quartered

8 large butter lettuce leaves
2 large limes, quartered
Sriracha sauce, to serve (optional)

SHAKIN' BACON

Frankie is another insanely talented chef at Artichoke. He's in charge of all the bigwigs: smoked chicken, roast lamb shoulder, etc. Frankie's Vietnamese, and came up with the idea of applying the principles of bo luc lac (Vietnamese 'shaking beef') to bacon. Bo luc lac gets its name from the tossing of beef cubes as they're stir-fried in a wok; this dish does the same to tender, cubed pieces of belly bacon.

»»»»

Heat a wok over medium-high heat. Throw in the bacon cubes (no need for oil here) and cook for 3 minutes, shaking the wok every 30 seconds. Add the onions and cook for 2 minutes more to slightly soften the onions. Transfer the bacon-onion mixture to a large mixing bowl and load it with all the Shakin' Mix ingredients. Toss well.

Divide the bacon across the lettuce leaves (which function as little 'cups'). Squeeze some lime juice and Sriracha sauce over each cup, bunch up the edges of the 'cups, and pop the whole thing in your mouth. *Explosion*.

EAT WITH ONE HAND

BLT FRIED RICE

2 tbsp vegetable oil

200 g slab belly bacon,
coarsely chopped into cubes

2 cloves garlic, finely chopped

2 stalks spring onion, finely chopped

2 eggs, beaten

4 cups jasmine rice, cooked the
previous day and chilled overnight

4 tbsp ketchup

4 tbsp light soy sauce,
plus additional for adjusting

1 tsp white pepper powder

At least ½ cup vegetable oil, for frying

4 eggs

½ head iceberg or romaine lettuce,
finely shredded

Maple syrup, for drizzling

BLT FRIED RICE
WITH WOK-FRIED EGGS AND MAPLE SYRUP

In tandem with the F1 Singapore Grand Prix week in 2013, Artichoke presented a week-long menu called 'Dude, Where's My Food' that featured an unapologetic array of bro-friendly food. Jim Beam, nachos, and a shit-ton of bacon made their way unto the plate. BLT (Bacon, Lettuce, Tomato) Fried Rice, a spinoff of BLT sandwiches, was one of the dishes we served. What's more dude-like than sitting in front of the TV, balancing a bowl on your stomach, and eating out of it with just one spoon? You don't even have to look down to eat. To regress one step further, we replaced tomatoes (the T in BLT) with ketchup. And topped the entire thing with a fried egg doused in maple syrup, because that is something we can't not do.

»»»»»

Heat up the oil in a wok over high heat. Add the bacon and fry for about 1 minute, or until browned on all sides. Throw in the garlic and spring onion and fry for 1 minute more, then pour in the eggs and scramble it good. Toss in the rice and stir-fry for 2 minutes to char the rice grains. Add the ketchup, soy sauce and pepper and cook for 2 minutes more. Season to taste with more soy sauce if you like. Remove from the wok and keep warm.

Wash the wok and heat it up again over high heat. Pour in the oil and when it's super hot, crack in an egg. Fry the egg, basting the top of it in hot oil for a minute till the bottom is crispy and the yolk is still nice and runny. Place on kitchen paper to absorb the oil and repeat with the other three eggs.

To serve, divide the lettuce across four plates, then top each with a bowlful of fried rice and a fried egg. Drizzle maple syrup, as much or as little as you like, over each fried egg.

What's more dude-like than sitting in front of the TV, balancing a bowl on your stomach, and eating out of it with just one spoon?

SWEETS FROM
Please see wh
have next
a little bit of this and
that, rather than 2
Same thing. Feel fr
once.

Jonathan explaining the idea behind the Mamee salad with homemade curry-infused Spam at Rock Out With Your Pork Out, a two-night, round-the-world edible homage to pork.

ROCK OUT WITH YOUR PORK OUT

SERVES
4

TUNA TARTARE WITH PORK CRACKLING,
EBIKO LABNEH AND SPICY NORI CUCUMBER

TUNA TARTARE

150 g sashimi-grade tuna,
    chopped into 1cm cubes
3 tbsp shoyu (Japanese light soy sauce)
½ tsp sugar
1 tbsp chopped chives
1 tbsp chopped Thai basil
1 shallot, thinly sliced into rings
1 tbsp extra virgin olive oil
1 tbsp white sesame seeds,
    toasted (page 19)
Salt and pepper

EBIKO LABNEH

3 tbsp ebiko (prawn roe)
    or tobiko (flying fish roe)
2 tbsp extra virgin olive oil
1 tbsp lemon juice
1 cup labneh (page 260)

SPICY NORI CUCUMBER

1 Lebanese or Japanese cucumber
2 tbsp nori harissa (page 231)
1 tbsp lemon juice
Salt and pepper

1 small bag store-bought
    pork crackling
1 handful garden cress or
    mixed baby herbs (if you can't
    find these readily in the market,
    go ahead and use sprouts:
    broccoli sprouts, radish or
    pea sprouts, alfalfa, etc.)
Extra virgin olive oil, for drizzling

We served this dish at Rock Out With Your Pork Out, a two-night lard-filled extravaganza. Raw tuna and pork crackling is another surf and turf iteration I love. Apart from providing a crunchy, flavourful counterpoint to the soft moistness of tuna, chicharrones is simply one of my favourite things in the world. Every time I hang out at Lucky Plaza (a Filipino-centric mall in Singapore), I'm enraptured by the bags of fried goodness hanging in stalls like ripe fruit. I never desist. If I could hang the damn things on my Christmas tree, I would. You could say this dish was just an opportunistic way of introducing chicharrones unto the menu. You'll be able to find them at most Filipino and Thai malls. In Singapore, that'll be Lucky Plaza and Golden Mile Complex.

»»»»

To make the tuna tartare, mix all ingredients in a large bowl and season further if necessary with salt and pepper. Place in the fridge for at least 2 hours, to allow the flavours to develop.

To make the ebiko labneh, simply mix the ebiko, olive oil and lemon juice into the labneh. Place in the fridge for at least 2 hours, to allow the flavours to develop.

While the tuna and ebiko labneh are chilling out in the fridge, smash the cucumber with something flat and heavy like a meat mallet or the plane of a cleaver. Chop the smashed cucumber up roughly. IMHO, smashing up the cucumber first makes the pieces rougher and more rustic than if you were to just chop it. Mix the cucumber with the harissa and lemon juice, and season to taste with salt and pepper.

To serve, smear a dollop of the ebiko labneh across a plate, then repeat for the next three plates. Top with the spicy cucumber and tuna tartare. Open your bag of pork cracklings and crush several pieces over the tuna. Garnish with the garden herbs and a drizzle of extra virgin olive oil.

ROCK OUT
WITH YOUR
PORK OUT

TAIWANESE SALT AND PEPPER PORK RIBS
WITH CENTURY EGG MAYO

PORK RIB MARINADE

1 tbsp finely chopped or grated garlic
2 tbsp sesame oil
2 tbsp vegetable oil
2 tbsp light soy sauce
1 tbsp sugar
4 tbsp Chinese cooking wine
1 tbsp coarsely ground white pepper
1 tsp sea salt
2 egg whites
6 tbsp rice flour
1 tsp bicarbonate of soda (optional)
1 kg pork baby back ribs, cut into
    individual ribs

CENTURY EGG MAYO

1 cup Japanese mayo (Kewpie brand)
2 century eggs, peeled and coarsely
    chopped
1 tbsp lemon juice
1 tbsp sesame oil
Salt and pepper

Vegetable oil, for deep-frying and
    frying
8 cloves garlic, finely chopped
½ red capsicum, chopped
½ green capsicum, chopped
¼ white onion, chopped
1 stalk spring onion, finely chopped
1 handful fresh coriander
1 tsp sea salt
1 tsp coarsely ground white pepper

Bruce, one of our hot-station boys, is a Taiwanese culinary school intern. His name isn't even Bruce at all; it's Bo Lin. But we decided to call him Bruce on day one and that was that. His dish for Rock Out With Your Pork Out is based on zhu pa (lightly breaded pork chops) served at Taipei's famous night markets. His stir-fried pork ribs are blanketed with a chunky, funky century egg mayo—tying the Taiwanese influence back to Artichoke's dude food philosophy.

»»»»»

To marinate the pork ribs, mix all the marinade ingredients together in a large bowl. The wet and dry ingredients should combine to become a wet paste that coats the ribs well. Rub the paste well into the ribs and allow them to marinate for at least 6 hours.

To make the century egg mayo, mix all the ingredients together and season to taste with salt and pepper.

When ready to cook, preheat the oil in a deep fryer to 180°C. If you do not have a deep fryer, heat 10cm of vegetable oil in a deep pot or saucepan over high heat till it reaches 180°C. When the oil is hot enough, place the ribs one by one into the oil and fry for about 4 minutes, or until the ribs are cooked through and the crust is golden-brown and crispy. Keep warm.

In a hot wok or deep frying pan, heat up 4 tablespoons of vegetable oil over medium-high heat. Once it starts to smoke, throw in the garlic, capsicums and onions and stir-fry for 30 seconds. Add the pork ribs to the wok and toss with the vegetables for 1 minute more. Turn off the heat and add in the spring onion, coriander, salt and pepper. Toss to combine.

Remove the ribs to a plate and dollop large spoonfuls of century egg mayo over them.

CHAPTER 14

Nothing Escapes the Fryer

»»»»

As with bacon, we have a sick obsession with throwing food into the fryer and seeing what happens. Anyone can deep-fry chicken nuggets and calamari, though; what I'm talking about here is the less obvious/predictable stuff. One signature dish at the restaurant is fried cauliflower with almonds and pomegranate.

People always ask how we make cauliflower taste so good. My simple answer: "We take a perfectly healthy vegetable and chuck it into the fryer." At that temperature (180°C), the insides of the vegetables are essentially steamed, becoming soft and juicy. The magic happens closer to the surface, as the sugars receive an intense caramelisation to become sweet, crispy, and even a little (ooh, yes) meaty.

We have a logbook documenting every vegetable we've deep-fried. We've done the research so you don't have to. The verdict on deep-fried carrots, Romanesco, Brussels sprouts, lotus roots, and wedges of cabbage—awesome. When you deep-fry an entire stalk of leek, it's all roasty on the outside and juicy in the middle. Broccoli morphs into an absolute beauty, the nooks and crannies of its florets serving as hyper-efficient absorbers of heat and oil. It ultimately tastes like crispy little pieces of fried chicken skin. Navy beans remain fluffy in the middle, as do chickpeas (they taste like little chicken nuggets). Basically anything in the brassica family—hard, dry vegetables—will taste tremendous after a few

We take a perfectly healthy vegetable and chuck it into the fryer.

minutes in hot oil. Ingredients with a surfeit of juice, like watermelon wedges and daikon, turn out totally sucky and flaccid. Don't do it.

Apart from vegetables, we've also experimented with mayonnaise that'd been frozen into cubes and coated with breadcrumbs. (They split in the fryer, unfortunately.) We've cracked raw eggs into the fryer, resulting in oil-soaked, crispy filigree. When soft-boiled eggs are deep-fried, their whites turn a little rubbery, bouncing their way around the insides of your mouth. But once you sink your teeth into the sucker the yolk bursts out with extra-explosive force. Fantastic.

The recipes here demonstrate how simple ingredients can achieve new levels of awesomeness just by taking a hot oil bath. We're not talking predictable things like fish fingers and potatoes. We're going left field with the unexpected—as I said, nothing escapes the fryer.

½ head large cauliflower, or 1 small one
Vegetable oil, for deep-frying
½ cup canned chickpeas, drained
Salt and pepper
¼ red onion, thinly sliced
1 tbsp raisins, soaked in water
   for 1 hour and drained
2 tbsp flaked almonds,
   toasted (page 19)
1 handful mint leaves, roughly torn
2 tbsp pomegranate arils

About 2 tbsp Pomegranate Vinaigrette
   (page 256)
Labneh Ranch Dressing,
   to serve (page 262)
Lemon wedges, to serve

DEEP-FRIED CAULIFLOWER
WITH ALMONDS AND LABNEH RANCH DRESSING

In the Middle East, cauliflower is commonly eaten roasted and served with a tahini dipping sauce. We wanted to get rid of the two-step process, to combine all the elements into a one-mouthful flavour bomb. So we threw in a jeweled garnish into the mix—chunks of onion, almonds, herbs, raisins and juicy pomegranate arils to accompany the deep-fried veggie, and spammed the whole mix with creamy labneh ranch. It kinda looks like Candy Crush, on a plate.

»»»»»

Cut the cauliflower into small florets. Preheat the oil in a deep fryer to 180°C. If you don't have a deep fryer, heat 10cm of vegetable oil in a deep pot or saucepan over high heat. To test if the oil is hot enough, throw in one floret. It should sizzle vigorously. Deep-fry the cauliflower florets and chickpeas for about 2 to 3 minutes, until they turn golden brown. Drain on kitchen paper and season well with salt and pepper.

To serve, toss the fried cauliflower in a bowl with the onion, raisins, almonds, mint and pomegranate arils. Dress with the vinaigrette. Smear the labneh ranch on a communal platter and place the cauliflower over. Top with an extra dollop or two of labneh ranch and lemon wedges to finish.

Vegetable oil, for deep-frying
2 cups canned chickpeas,
    rinsed and dried
1 cup plain flour
2 tsp ras el hanout (page 30)
1 tsp smoked paprika
1 tsp clear honey
1 small shallot, thinly sliced
½ handful fresh herbs
    (such as chives, scallions,
    mint, etc.), finely chopped
Sea salt flakes
Saffron Mayo (page 255)
Lemon wedges, to serve

DEEP-FRIED CHICKPEAS
WITH RAS EL HANOUT AND SAFFRON MAYO

Chickpeas are one of those things that, when taken on a trip to Fry Town and back, end up tasting like round little French fries. That's because while their skins crisp up in the hot oil, their insides become soft and fluffy. The chickpeas, ras el hanout and saffron elements make this a really Moroccan-centric dish that's a great sidekick to a piece of grilled fish or a roast shoulder of lamb (page 119).

»»»»

Preheat the oil in your deep fryer to 180°C. If you don't have a deep fryer, heat 10cm of vegetable oil in a deep pot or saucepan over high heat till it reaches 180°C. Toss the chickpeas in the flour and pour them into a colander to shake off the excess flour. Deep-fry the chickpeas for 3 to 4 minutes till crispy on the outside. Immediately toss them into a mixing bowl with the ras el hanout, paprika, honey, shallots and herbs. Season to taste with sea salt. Scoop onto a serving platter and drizzle generously with the mayo. Throw on a couple of lemon wedges and serve hot.

When taken on a trip to Fry Town and back, chickpeas end up tasting like round little French fries.

WHIPPED FETA
100 g soft feta
100 g plain yoghurt
1 tsp dried mint or dill
1 tbsp extra virgin olive oil
Pinch of black pepper,
    plus additional for adjusting
Salt

Vegetable oil, for deep-frying
200 g Brussels sprouts, halved
1 tbsp lemon juice
1 tbsp clear honey
1 handful mint leaves
1 shallot, thinly sliced into rings
Salt and pepper
2 tbsp hazelnuts, toasted and
    coarsely chopped (page 19)

DEEP-FRIED BRUSSELS SPROUTS
WITH HONEY, WHIPPED FETA AND HAZELNUTS

The whipped feta here—comprising feta and yoghurt—provides a cooling, smooth counterpoint to the delicious charred intensity of the Brussels sprouts, as well as Middle Eastern-izes things up a bit. Use Persian or Danish feta, which is softer. Try not to use Greek or Australian feta, as it is firm and crumbly, and thus less suitable for whipping. Remember to remove the darker outer leaves of the sprouts before deep-frying.

>>>>>

To make the whipped feta, beat the feta in a mixing bowl with the other ingredients. Season to taste.

Preheat the oil in a deep fryer to 180°C. If you don't have a deep fryer, heat 10cm of vegetable oil in a deep pot or saucepan over high heat. To test if the oil is hot enough, throw in one sprout. It should sizzle vigorously. Deep-fry the Brussels sprouts for about 1½ minutes, or until they turn brown and crinkled. Remove and drain on kitchen paper. Toss with the lemon juice, honey, mint and shallots. Season well with salt and pepper.

To serve, spread some whipped feta on a plate. Top with the Brussels sprouts, then scatter the hazelnuts to finish.

EAT WITH
BARE
HANDS

BRAISED DUCK WINGS

1 kg duck wings, chopped into
    drumlets and winglets
1 yellow onion, halved
1 thumb-sized piece ginger
5 cloves garlic
2 bay leaves
1 tbsp coriander seeds,
    toasted (page 19)
1 cinnamon stick
1 star anise
2 tbsp brown sugar
1 tbsp salt

CUMIN SALT

2 tbsp cumin seeds, toasted
2 tbsp smoked sea salt
1 tsp MSG powder (optional)

Vegetable oil, for deep-frying
2 cups corn flour, for dusting
Lime wedges, for serving

CRISPY DUCK WINGS
WITH CUMIN SALT AND LIME

A lot of the food at Artichoke is inspired by what we eat on our days off. One late night, I found some duck wings in my fridge left there by my granddad. He used to love duck wings braised Teochew-style in a dark soy sauce. So what did I do? Deep-fry them, of course. Duh. Braising the wings before frying is important, because they'll be too stringy and dry otherwise. To get raw duck wings, just pop by any wet market in Singapore. However, if you're too lazy to braise your own wings, just buy them from any hawker stall specialising in Teochew braised duck.

〉〉〉〉〉

Place the duck wings and all the braising ingredients into a stockpot, and add just enough water to submerge the ingredients. Bring to a gentle simmer and cook, covered, for 2 hours or until the meat is fall-apart tender.

Now for the make-it-or-break-it part of the recipe. Allow the wings to cool to room temperature in their braising liquid as this will allow them to retain maximum moisture. If you pull them out of the braising liquid while hot, the meat will dry up and become stringy. When totally cool, remove the wings carefully and place them in a colander to drip dry. The meat is super tender right now, so work gently to avoid accidentally ripping meat off the bones.

To make the cumin salt, coarsely grind the cumin seeds in a pestle and mortar. Then add the salt and MSG powder and grind again.

Preheat your deep fryer to 185°C. If you don't have a deep fryer, heat 10cm of vegetable oil in a deep pot or saucepan over high heat till it reaches 185°C. Coat each winglet or drumlet with the corn flour and shake off the excess. Deep-fry in the hot oil for 2 minutes. Remove from the oil and toss in the cumin salt. Serve with lime wedges.

CHAPTER 15

Every Day I Die a Little

>>>>>>

I **love my job, really I do. If I hadn't risked it all on this restaurant, I'd have spent the rest of my sad, disillusioned life wondering what would have happened if I did. The way I see it is, if you've got it in your blood, there's no getting it out.**

When I was four, I told my mom my life's goal was to be a 'rice cooker', which was my infantile conception of working with food at the time. To further ~~exploit~~ encourage my professed interest, she handed me a pot of rice to wash for as long as I wanted. Half an hour later, dear mother's jasmine rice resembled Vietnamese broken rice instead. Oops.

At the age of seven, when I was living with my grandparents, the constant parade of porridge and prune juice so depressed me that I was forced to rustle up my first dish: a mongrel meatloaf. I pulled out a can of Vienna sausages from the cupboard, smashed them up with a fork, mixed in some MacDonald's chilli sauce straight from the sachet, stirred in eggs and corn flour, and cooked the damn thing secretly in a pan. It probably tasted like shit, but I ate it anyway. My lucky third aunt got a taste, and she was blown away. (Probably for the sole reason that I was only seven.)

Yes, I can die happy tomorrow, knowing that I've accomplished one of the major things I want to do with my life.

But. Every time someone says to me "Oh, you're so lucky; you own your own restaurant. You're doing what you love. I think I'd love to do that too, one day", I gun them down. I gun them down hard. I don't mean to be an asshole. But they deserve to know the truth about what life is like as the chef-owner of a restaurant:

It probably tasted like shit, but I ate it anyway.

Things we do at Artichoke to make ourselves feel better:

1. Concocting a Spam, Mamee and egg salad and serving the damn thing in a wine glass.

2. Intense ball grabs. Frequency of grabs increases after 9pm.

3. Shaving cheese into Mark's open mouth, just because.

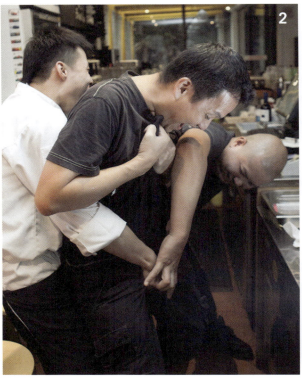

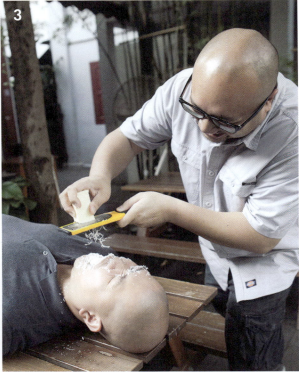

Rest days? What rest days?

Many restaurants close one day a week, often on a Sunday or Monday. After working 72 or more hours the past six days, all you wanna do is fucking sleep. Well, good luck with that, because there are a ton of things you gotta do on this most precious of days: buy teapots to replace those that broke over the weekend, call one insurance company to follow up on a claim, call another to follow up on a different claim, clarify mysterious payments due with the accountants, pay the two parking fines on the company van, bank in the week's cash sales, answer the phone that still rings 20 times an hour, etc. Even if you stop yourself from doing these things because you're supposed to be resting, they'll continue to weigh heavily on your mind. (Plus they'll pile up even more by tomorrow.)

You're especially screwed if your rest day is a Monday. That's because Monday is the first day of the week for everyone else, and they're all well rested and geared up for action. What's more, they had two days over the weekend to store up a bunch of questions and/or requests that they unload on you first thing Monday morning.

So, good luck getting any fucking 'rest'.

Bodily needs and functions take a back seat

You eat your lunch at 5pm, have dinner at midnight, sleep at 3am, and wake up at 10am, only to find **77 missed calls, 5 SMSes and 39 Whatsapp messages on your phone**. Half of them are urgent; the remaining half will ask you to do something 'at your convenience' which essentially means 'by today, please'.

At 4pm, you need to pee. With constant interruptions by people and situations that require immediate attention, you end up peeing at 6pm. While you're peeing, your phone continues to vibrate incessantly in your pocket.

Catastrophes occur daily

Expect one major disaster every day. Its severity will range from the dishwasher calling in sick on a Friday, to the air-conditioner duct exploding and spraying water all over the poor people at Table 6, to the exhaust system malfunctioning in the middle of a Saturday night slam, choking everyone in the kitchen and dining room with smoke from the charcoal grill. The impossible can and will happen, like a sudden shower of caterpillars from the sky (no kidding), or a marathon of rats emerging from underground and running across your courtyard in the middle of Saturday brunch because government pest control forgot to seal the street openings across the restaurant while exterminating the critters in the sewers (also true).

Human relationships take a hit

Your loved ones can't understand your troubles. If they ever do, it'll probably take a long time. You'll be lucky if you don't fall out with them in the meantime. They won't understand why you're always so stressed out; why you are an alcoholic or chain smoker; why you can't just take a break when you need one. Without meaning any harm, they'll ask insensitive questions like those you get from nasty customers: "How hard can it be to pee when you need to pee?" or "I don't understand why you can't find time to have proper meals".

As for the customers—don't expect them to cut you any slack either. They see the restaurant as a machine that delivers food, drink and service, not as the collective efforts of humans who have personalities, feelings and bladders. And it's through no fault of theirs. So in the middle of a Friday night slam, they can't—and shouldn't—be told that all food orders will be held back by 5 minutes because the head chef really needs to use the loo.

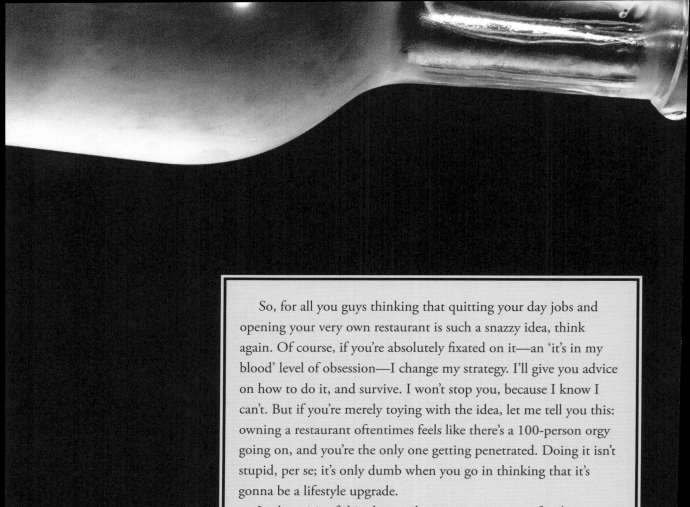

So, for all you guys thinking that quitting your day jobs and opening your very own restaurant is such a snazzy idea, think again. Of course, if you're absolutely fixated on it—an 'it's in my blood' level of obsession—I change my strategy. I'll give you advice on how to do it, and survive. I won't stop you, because I know I can't. But if you're merely toying with the idea, let me tell you this: owning a restaurant oftentimes feels like there's a 100-person orgy going on, and you're the only one getting penetrated. Doing it isn't stupid, per se; it's only dumb when you go in thinking that it's gonna be a lifestyle upgrade.

In the spirit of this chapter, here are some recipes for days when you're dying inside and just want to end your life with some heart-stopping food.

ARTICHOKE FRIED CHICKEN

WITH HONEY LEMON BUTTER AND TAHINI COLESLAW

Our infamous brunch dish that's a mash-up between Southern fried chicken and Lebanese shish taouk (chicken kebabs). To keep the dish pointed towards Lebanon, we use a shish taouk-inspired marinade to coat the chicken before deep-frying, and serve toum as a dip. If the Koreans have their sweet soy glaze, and the Americans their maple syrup, why not coat our finished product with a Middle Eastern-flavoured equivalent—honey lemon butter? At Artichoke, each order comes with three staggering pieces of chicken, a heaped mound of coleslaw, pickles and enough garlic-spiked toum to send your significant other reeling. If you haven't guessed by now, the point of this insanely excessive dish is simply to stick a middle finger to life.

BRINE

2 litres water
½ cup kosher salt
½ cup brown sugar
1 lemon, halved
5 cloves garlic, smashed
1 tbsp black peppercorns, crushed
2 bay leaves
2 green cardamom pods, crushed
1 cinnamon stick
2 medium chickens (ask your butcher to chop each into wings, breasts, thighs and drumsticks)

SHISH TAOUK MARINADE

2 onions, juiced*
6 cloves garlic, finely chopped
¼ cup olive oil
2 tbsp chilli powder
1 tbsp cumin powder
1 tbsp coriander powder
1 cup plain yoghurt
1 tsp sea salt

HONEY LEMON BUTTER

100 g unsalted butter
150 g clear honey
1 handful finely chopped spring onion
1 tbsp lemon juice

*To juice an onion, blend one cup of water to one large onion in a liquidiser or food processor. Strain the onion smoothie, keeping the liquid and discarding the pulp.

»»»»»

To make the brine, combine all the ingredients (except the chicken) in a large pot or bucket and stir to dissolve the salt and sugar. Add the chicken pieces to the brine and allow to sit for exactly 6 hours—no more, no less. Remove the chicken from the brine, rinse well under running water and pat dry with kitchen paper.

Mix all the shish taouk marinade ingredients together in a bowl and add the chicken. Rub the mixture in thoroughly and allow to marinate for at least 6 hours more.

To make the honey lemon butter, place the butter and honey in a saucepan and bring to a heavy boil. Remove from the heat and add in the spring onions and lemon juice. Allow to cool to room temperature.

When ready to cook the chicken, remove the chicken pieces from the marinade and allow the excess marinade to drip off. Coat each piece heavily in plain flour. Transfer the pieces to a tray and allow to sit at room temperature for at least 10 minutes. This helps to 'temper' the meat, meaning it'll cook quicker and more evenly. This resting period also gives the flour time to adhere to the meat, thereby forming a better crust. »

TAHINI COLESLAW

1 cup shredded red cabbage

1 cup shredded white cabbage

½ red onion, thinly sliced

1 tbsp tahini

1 tbsp white sesame seeds,
    toasted (page 19)

2 tbsp Japanese mayonnaise
    (Kewpie brand)

1 tbsp lemon juice

1 tbsp extra virgin olive oil

Salt and pepper

Plain flour, for coating

Vegetable oil, for deep-frying

Artichoke-style Pickles,
    to serve (page 257)

Toum, to serve (page 253)

Toum Fries, to serve (optional, page 57)

While the chicken is resting, make the tahini coleslaw. Mix all the ingredients in a large bowl. Season well with salt and pepper. Keep chilled.

Preheat the vegetable oil in a deep fryer to 170°C. If you don't have a deep fryer, heat 10cm of vegetable oil in a deep pot or saucepan over medium heat till it reaches 170°C. When the oil is hot enough, cook the chicken in small batches for about 6 minutes on each side. Note that breasts and wings cook faster, while thighs and drumsticks require a little more time to cook through. It's worth sacrificing a piece to test for doneness—simply take it out and cut into it with a knife to check.

Remove and immediately toss the pieces in a large mixing bowl with the honey lemon butter. Divide the chicken pieces across four plates and serve with bowls of coleslaw, pickles, toum and fries to pass round the table.

EAT SHAMELESSLY

PICKLE RELISH

1 handful Sichuan chye (pickled
  Sichuan preserved vegetables),
  finely chopped
1 tbsp kana chye (preserved olive leaf)
1 large tomato, finely chopped
1 stalk spring onion, chopped
1 handful fresh coriander, chopped
1 tbsp rice wine vinegar
1 tbsp sesame oil
1 tbsp oyster sauce
2 tbsp extra virgin olive oil

1 ham chim peng
  (savoury Chinese 'donut')
1 tsp hoisin sauce
1 handful iceberg lettuce,
  finely shredded
3 siew mai (steamed pork dumplings)
  from your friendly convenience store
  or coffee shop
Century Egg Mayo,
  to garnish (page 171)

The burger goes down smooth
with some Chinese New Year
Ginger Beer (page 155).

HAM CHIM PENG BURGER
WITH CENTURY EGG MAYO AND PICKLE RELISH

I can't explain myself on this one. I came up with this hare-brained idea for an event proposal, the theme of which was Sports Day at School. What came to mind were fried foods in clear plastic bags; oil and grease; hand-held snacks brought down to the bleachers and eaten under a hot sun. Things like youtiao, curry puffs, siew mai, char siew bao, ham chim peng. This amazing monstrosity was the result of madly pulling together a bunch of canteen foods. We never served it, but it tastes awesome anyway.

»»»»

To make the pickle relish, mix all the ingredients in a bowl and allow to sit for at least 15 minutes to allow the flavours to mingle.

Split the ham chin peng in half like a burger bun. Spread the hoisin sauce on the bottom bun and top with a mound of iceberg lettuce. Place 3 siew mais over the lettuce and spoon some relish and egg mayo over the top. Place the top bun on and mow into this sucker.

2 large eggs

¼ cup heavy cream

1 tbsp unsalted butter, plus
   1 additional tbsp for the 'magic'

1 tbsp olive oil

Salt and pepper

1 thick slice of bread (preferably
   sourdough or ciabatta), toasted

BUTTER-WHIPPED SCRAMBLED EGGS

How do you make scrambled eggs any better than they already are? By doing like the French do and whipping in unnecessarily large amounts of butter. Monter au beurre, they call it. This aerates the eggs and fluffs them up, while rendering them richer and creamier at the same time. Whipping the eggs right out of the pan also dissipates excess heat, so the eggs stop cooking internally and remain slightly runny.

»»»»

In a mixing bowl, whisk the eggs with the heavy cream. Do not season it at this stage! Place a non-stick frying pan over medium heat. Add 1 tablespoon of the butter and the olive oil. When the butter starts to froth, turn the heat down to low, add the eggs and keep stirring with a flexible silicone spatula. As the egg curds start to set in a thin layer, scrape them off the surface of the pan. Allow new egg batter to flow to those newly exposed pan surfaces and repeat the process of scraping and mixing till the mixture is about 80 per cent solid. Immediately remove from the heat and dump the whole lot into a large, metallic mixing bowl. This process helps to knock out the excess heat in the eggs, and prevents it from overcooking in its residual heat.

Working quickly, throw the rest of the butter and a pinch of salt in with the eggs. Beat the life out of the eggs to show them who's boss. Once the butter has been whipped in completely, taste it and season with more salt and pepper to your liking. If you wanna be fancy, now's the time to fold in fancy things like truffle oil and chopped herbs. I'm a caveman and so I like to keep mine basic. Serve immediately on the hot toast. You won't believe what this simple technique can do to elevate your humble scrammies.

"Owning a restaurant oftentimes feels like there's a 100-person orgy going on, and you're the only one getting penetrated."

YOUTIAO HOTDOG

1 stick youtiao (Chinese cruller),
  cut to the length of your sausage

1 cooked sausage of your liking

**A VARIETY OF TOPPINGS—
  TAKE YOUR PICK**

Yellow mustard

Sauerkraut

Coleslaw

Any type of raw onions, thinly sliced

Dill pickles

Cheez Whiz

Japanese mayonnaise (Kewpie brand)

Sriracha

Roasted Eggplant Relish (page 263)

Saffron Mayo (page 255)

Toum (page 253)

Tahini Coleslaw (page 188)

Just like the Char Siew Bao Grilled Sandwiches (page 110), the Youtiao (Chinese cruller) Hotdog idea just hit me one day. It's as if aliens penetrated my head and planted crop circles of ridiculous youtiao permutations on the fallow field of my brain. Consider this: whoever invented the youtiao must have stuck two long strips of dough together for a reason, so why the hell are we pulling them apart to eat? Consider the intentions of this person carefully, and you'll see that he or she created the perfect sausage-holding vessel but was probably too shy to say it. Now that we've figured it out, it's time to do the right thing. The version you see here comprises a Johnsonville cheese bratwurst, an impossible mound of tahini coleslaw (page 188) and a generous squirt of Sriracha. Be sure to use only straight sausages for this recipe so they nestle well into the youtiao groove.

»»»»»

All you have to do is nestle the sausage into the convenient groove between the two dough strips and go crazy with the toppings of your choice!

Like a few other dishes in this book, this is more of an idea than a recipe. I'd like to imagine that you're by now totally blown away by it and are already churning out possible combinations in your head. Here are some permutations to get you started: »

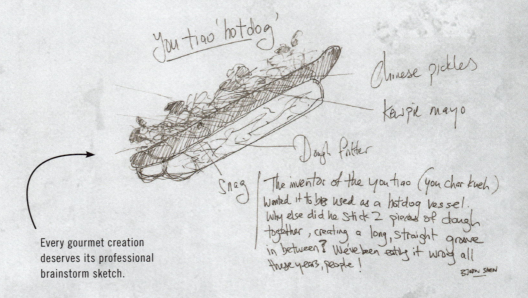

You tiao 'hotdog'

Chinese pickles

Kewpie mayo

Dough fritter

Snag

The inventor of the youtiao (you char kueh) wanted it to be used as a hotdog vessel. Why else did he stick 2 pieces of dough together, creating a long, straight groove in between? We've been eating it wrong all these years, people!

BJORN SHEN

Every gourmet creation deserves its professional brainstorm sketch.

My Fantasy 'Dog of the Moment: cheese bratwurst + coleslaw + roasted eggplant relish + Sriracha sauce

Mexican 'Dog: pork sausage + pork carnitas + guacamole + queso fresco + pico de gallo

Breakfast 'Dog: breakfast sausage + bacon + scrambled eggs + maple syrup

Indian 'Dog: spicy lamb sausage + chickpea daal + tandoori paneer + mint chutney

Now go dream up yours.

ROCK OUT
WITH YOUR
PORK OUT

SERVES
1

MAMEE SALAD
WITH SPAM AND EGG

In the same vein as the Artichoke Fried Chicken (page 188), this recipe is also a middle finger to salads everywhere. Which 10-year-old, or juvenile grown-ass man, doesn't like a dish that's salty, crunchy and artificially flavoured? 'Nuff said.

SALAD
½ handful shredded napa cabbage
½ handful shredded red cabbage
½ handful fresh herbs (such as coriander, mint, parsley, basil, etc.)
1 small shallot, thinly sliced
Vegetable oil, for frying
1 bag instant ramen or ready-to-eat crispy noodle snacks (such as Mamee Noodle Snack)
1 tbsp Pomegranate Vinaigrette (page 256)
1 tbsp Labneh Ranch Dressing (page 262)

2 thick slices Spam or luncheon meat
Vegetable oil, for frying
1 large egg
Wedge of lime, to serve
1 tbsp extra virgin olive oil, for drizzling

》》》》》

To make the salad, place the napa cabbage, red cabbage, herbs and shallots in a large mixing bowl and toss to combine. Heat 2.5 to 3cm of vegetable oil in a heavy-based frying pan over high heat, then rip open the bag of ramen and deep-fry the whole block of noodles till golden and crispy. Allow to cool slightly, then crumble into the bowl. If you're using ready-to-eat noodle snacks (which I wholeheartedly recommend), just crumble the block of noodles straight into the bowl. Open the sachet of seasoning powder that comes with the noodles and sprinkle half of it into the bowl (or all of it if you're not pretending to be healthy—MSG for the win!). Dress the salad with the vinaigrette and ranch dressing. Set aside.

Fry your Spam in some vegetable oil till done to your liking. Some like it barely seared and super juicy, some like it overdone and crispy. (I like mine sort of 75 per cent crispy.) Cook your egg to your liking – you can boil or fry it. I like mine soft-boiled, with a really explosive, runny yolk as in our Quick Butter Bean Ful (page 59).

To finish, slice the Spam into smaller pieces and toss through the salad. Pile up the salad on a plate, top with the egg and a wedge of lime, and drizzle with the extra virgin olive oil.

'FISH 'N CHIPS'
WITH 'BLACK TAR'

'BLACK TAR', I.E. SQUID INK TARTAR SAUCE

1 cup Japanese mayonnaise (Kewpie brand)

2 tbsp capers, finely chopped

2 tbsp finely chopped gherkins or cornichons

2 tbsp finely chopped shallots

1 tbsp finely chopped fresh dill

1 tsp or one small sachet squid ink

1 tbsp lemon juice

2 tbsp vegetable oil, for frying

4 fillets red snapper (about 200 g each), skin on

Sea salt and coarsely ground black pepper

2 cups crushed salt and vinegar-flavoured potato chips

2 tbsp finely chopped chives

4 lemon wedges

For Dude Food week, I wanted to change up the boring old schtick of beer-battered fish and chips. So we pan-seared a few good slabs of fish and sprinkled them liberally with crushed salt and vinegar potato chips. (Lay's is my preferred brand.) Voila. To dude things up a little more, we added the element of 'black tar'—tartar sauce jacked up with the briny hint of squid ink. Plus, it's black. That's always cool. You'll be able to find squid ink in gourmet grocers; they come either in jars or little sachets (each of which is roughly equivalent to 1 tsp). The recipe yields about 1½ cups of tartar sauce, which will keep for 3 days in the fridge.

»»»»

To make the tartar sauce, mix all the ingredients well in a bowl and set aside.

To cook the fish, heat up the oil in a non-stick frying pan over medium heat. Season the fish fillets with the salt and pepper on both sides. Place the fillets in the pan, skin side down. After 3 minutes, flip the fillets and cook for 1 minute more, or until the fish is cooked through. You can tell it's cooked if you poke a fork into it and it goes straight through without any resistance.

To serve, spread 1 tablespoon of tartar sauce onto each of four plates. Place a fillet over the sauce and top with the crushed potato crisps. Sprinkle the chives over each fillet and pop a wedge of lemon next to it. Hand those plates out and watch them get destroyed.

To dude things up a little more, we added the element of 'black tar' —tartar sauce jacked up with the briny hint of squid ink. Plus, it's black. That's always cool.

Artichoke Abroad

»»»»»

Working in the hospitality industry means that we work A LOT and can rarely afford to take long periods of leave. What's worse, during holiday periods when our family and friends are planning their vacations, it's major slam season for us.

Travel exposes us to new cultures, cuisines, people, and the occasional icky delicacy.

That said, I believe very strongly in the value of travel. To be good service providers, we first have to be well-exposed, well seasoned consumers.

For this reason, we close the restaurant at least once a year so the whole crew can go overseas together on a company retreat. During this one week, we keep things free and easy, but I encourage everyone to check out as many places as their daily travel allowances and stomachs will permit. The fellas go everywhere...

MELBOURNE, 2011

We checked out farmers' markets; sipped on fantastic coffees at little lane-way cafes in the Central Business District; hoovered up freekeh salads and carrots with harissa and almond cream at Cumulus Inc.; went to town on pinchos at buzzy tapas joint MoVida Aqui; dug into bowls of pho and plates of broken rice at scruffy Vietnamese eateries in Richmond.

BANGKOK, 2012

We hit up the streets of Sukhumvit and ate fried crickets, boat noodles and sausages of dubious origin; indulged in the best green curry (of salted wagyu beef, no less) I've ever had at Bo.lan; lapped up hummus, shawarma and baklava by the roadside in Soi Arab in between foot massages and nail spas.

Clockwise from top left: Singaporean Street Food Festival, Copenhagen; filming with the United Nations in Ben Tre, Vietnam; serving hungry customers; Danes trying out Singaporean fare; conducting a Progressive Singaporean Cuisine class at Claus Meyer's Madhus, Copenhagen; Ron attacking monster crackling in Copenhagen.

SYDNEY, 2013

We scarfed down curbside meat pies and mystery tacos at El Loco; feasted on a mind-bending dessert of caramelised pork shoulder drenched in caramel at Momofuku Seiōbo; stuffed our faces with gorgeous pastries from Black Star Bakery and Bourke Street Bakery; enjoyed mussel escabeche and fish fingers feathered with mojama shavings at Bodega; devoured fish and chips on Bondi Beach; ducked in and out of Lebanese bakeries and charcoal chicken shops in Granville; visited artisan producers of jams, cheeses and chocolates on the South Coast.

COPENHAGEN, 2013

Roxanne, two Artichoke sous chefs and I flew to Copenhagen with the Singapore Tourism Board to participate in the Copenhagen Cooking Festival. When we weren't slinging out Bak Chor Mee Sandwiches (page 208) and raw fish salads (page 211) from a food stall in Vesterbro Square, we hunted down the city's best smørrebrød; tried to achieve greatness through osmosis by sniffing the godly garbage at the back of Noma; got mugged by street punks; chased these street punks down and put them in choke holds; dug into great seafood, reindeer moss and smoked buttermilk panna cotta at Kødbyens Fiskebar in the old meatpacking district.

HO CHI MINH CITY, 2014

We braved the heat and sought out life-changing banh mi in the street food heaven of Saigon District 4; destroyed plates of barbecued seafood—fish, clams, all manner of unknown shells and alien-like critters—at open-air roadside stalls; slurped up endless bowls of bun bo hue and hu tieu at anonymous street stands; devoured charcoal-grilled goat nipples* at a locals-only joint in District 7; washed it all down with cool avocado smoothies.

Each new city we visited gave us new insights and inspiration. As hospitality professionals, we're not just here to put food on the table. We can be a lot more, and we want to be a lot more. Travel exposes us to new cultures, cuisines, people and the occasional icky delicacy, furnishing a richness of experience that we then transfer to the plates at Artichoke.

Facing page, anti-clockwise from top: Ban xeo on the streets of Phan Thiet; eating with the crew in Ho Chi Minh City; street side chicks; Artichoke boys arriving at Claus Meyer's central kitchen for prep. This page, clockwise from left: Local market in Ben Tre; digging into a family lunch with locals; Artichoke loves Sydney.

*You must be wondering what a goat's nipple tastes like. It is, I kid you not, milky, almost like haloumi. The meat is silky, hovering somewhere between cooked pork fat and tuna belly sashimi. Milky bits of fat also squish out when you bite in. It's weird, but I kinda like it.

BAK CHOR FILLING

Vegetable oil, for frying

500 g minced pork (try to steer
  away from the lean variety—
  the fattier the better)

5 cloves garlic, finely chopped

5 pieces dried shiitake mushrooms,
  soaked overnight and thinly sliced

2 cups reserved shiitake mushroom
  soaking liquid

2 tbsp light soya sauce

2 tbsp fish sauce

2 tbsp oyster sauce

2 tbsp tomato ketchup

4 tbsp Chinese black vinegar

1 tsp white pepper

1 tbsp corn flour mixed
  with 3 tbsp water

1 stalk spring onion, finely chopped

1 handful fresh coriander, chopped

SPICY MAYO

Japanese mayonnaise (Kewpie brand)

Sriracha sauce (or any other brand
  of garlic chilli sauce)

2 bunches fresh egg noodles (about
  70 g) or 2 packets instant ramen*

12 Chinese steamed buns (or any
  soft white buns if unavailable)

12 leaves butter lettuce

*Deep-frying instant noodles is
a good alternative if you can't
find fresh egg noodles
in the market.

BAK CHOR MEE SANDWICH

While representing Singapore during the Copenhagen Cooking Festival in 2013, I came up with two modern interpretations of local dishes. In line with the Danish culture of eating salads and sandwiches for lunch, I created a similar combination with a local twist: a raw fish salad (page 211) and Bak Chor Mee (minced meat noodles) Sandwich. The idea of such a sandwich had been bandied about for a while by me and Ming Xuan (my pal and Rox's cousin); it's actually his idea and lifelong dream. The idea was simple: to translate the elements in a bowl of noodles into a sandwich. Minced meat, cooked local-style, became the sandwich filling, while 'noodles' came in the form of deep-fried egg noodles, crushed and sprinkled on top as a crispy garnish.

》》》》》

To make the meat filling, heat 2 tablespoons of vegetable oil in a frying pan over high heat. Fry the minced pork in batches for 4 minutes per batch, breaking the clumps up as you go. Set aside. In a large saucepan, heat some vegetable oil over medium-high heat. Add the garlic and fry till golden-brown. Add in the mushrooms, mushroom soaking liquid, soy sauce, fish sauce, oyster sauce, ketchup, vinegar and pepper. Bring to a simmer and cook for 1 hour, or until the mushrooms are tender. Add the cooked pork mince into the mushroom mix and braise for 5 minutes more. Thicken the liquid with the corn flour and water mixture till the filling is still moist but no longer runny. Stir in the spring onions and coriander. Set aside and keep warm. 》

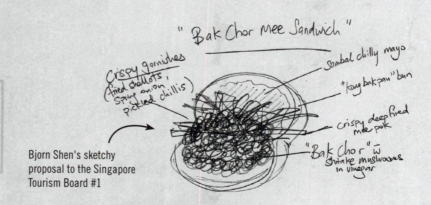

Bjorn Shen's sketchy proposal to the Singapore Tourism Board #1

» To make the spicy mayo, mix the mayonnaise and chilli sauce in any ratio to your preference. We like us some heat, so we usually go with 1 part mayonnaise to 2 parts chilli sauce.

Heat 10cm of vegetable oil in a deep pot or saucepan over high heat, then deep-fry the bunches of noodles till golden and crispy.

To serve, heat the buns in a steamer or microwave. Place a lettuce leaf at the base of each bun. Top this with a heaped tablespoon of the warm pork filling. Spoon on some spicy mayo. Break the crispy noodles into short lengths, scatter over the filling, and enclose the sandwich. Enjoy.

*When we were in Copenhagen, we made lime jelly 'pearls' by slowly dripping warm lime agar solution into ice-cold olive oil, which makes each drop set immediately in a spherical shape. It ends up looking like white caviar, complementing the whole seafood theme of the dish. If you're adventurous, try this at home.

SERVES 4

SOY DRESSING

4 tbsp light soya sauce

½ tbsp white sugar

½ tbsp white pepper powder

6 tbsp water

1 tbsp vegetable oil

Juice of 1 large lime, or about 1½ tbsp
  lime juice

4 tbsp sesame oil

LIME JELLY *

1 part lime juice to 1 part water
  (measurements will be based on the
  instructions on the agar packet)

Sugar, to taste

1 single serve packet (about 13 g) agar
  agar powder

½ cup puffed rice or Rice Krispies

1 tbsp sesame oil

200 g fresh toman (snakehead) or ikan
  parang (wolf herring) fish fillets

2 cups shredded iceberg lettuce

¼ large red onion, thinly sliced

1 large red chilli, thinly sliced

1 stalk spring onion, finely chopped

1 handful fresh coriander leaves

1 tsp white sesame seeds, toasted
  (page 19)

1 heaped tbsp crispy fried shallots
  (store-bought or prepared fresh)

SINGAPORE
RAW FISH SALAD 2013

The second dish we served in Copenhagen. The idea sprang from my favourite underdog Singaporean dish: porridge accompanied by raw fish salad. Unlike the much-publicized Chinese New Year version (page 157), this traditional dish is a humble mix of raw sliced wolf herring, drizzled with sesame oil, soy sauce and topped with spring onions, sliced chilli and coriander. We added a modern twist with lime pearls for an acidic pop, and the Rice Krispies were a sly allusion to the porridge this dish is usually served with.

»»»»

To make the dressing, combine all the ingredients in a glass jar and shake well.

To make the lime jelly, mix the lime juice and water together, then sweeten to taste with the sugar. Follow the manufacturer's instructions on the agar packet, adding in the slightly sweetened lime juice to result in lime-flavoured agar. Set the agar in a small bowl or tray and cut into 1cm cubes.

Put the puffed rice in a dry frying pan and stir frequently over medium-high heat for 2 minutes, or until it turns golden-brown. Drizzle in the sesame oil, give the rice a final quick stir and set aside to cool.

When ready to serve, slice the fish fillets as thinly as you can and lightly coat the slices with the soy dressing. Lay out the fish on individual serving plates or on a large communal platter. Toss the iceberg lettuce, onion, chilli, spring onion and coriander in a bowl and heap over the fish slices. Scatter with the toasted puffed rice, sesame seeds, crispy shallots, lime jelly and the remaining soy dressing.

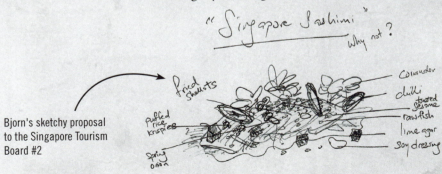

"Singapore Sashimi" why not?

Bjorn's sketchy proposal to the Singapore Tourism Board #2

ANCHOVY SAUCE

2 fillets salted anchovies

2 cloves garlic, peeled

2 egg yolks

2 tbsp Dijon mustard

4 tbsp white wine vinegar, plus
additional for adjusting

300 ml vegetable or sunflower oil,
plus additional for adjusting

1 tbsp lemon juice

Salt

PICKLED GARLIC

15 to 20 cloves garlic,
sliced very thinly

1 cup white wine vinegar

1 cup white sugar

1 cup water

Generous pinch of salt

Olive oil, for frying

1 head broccoli,
cut into small florets

Salt and pepper

1 red chilli, thinly sliced

1 to 2 tbsp unsalted butter

CHARRED BROCCOLI
WITH ANCHOVY SAUCE AND PICKLED GARLIC

This dish is infamous for converting broccoli haters at Artichoke. During our trip to Melbourne in 2011, Kel and I found the restaurants there treating their vegetables in a way that hadn't taken root in Singapore: charring them raw, straight in a frying pan or on the grill. Specifically, it was at Cumulus where we had amazing charred romanesco in a lemon emulsion. Dry cooking a vegetable over high heat, like a steak, caramelises its natural sugars and develops a fantastic flavour, without overcooking it on the inside. The recipe for anchovy sauce produces more than is necessary for this dish; the remainder can keep for 1 week in the fridge.

》》》》》

To make the anchovy sauce, place the anchovies, garlic, yolks, mustard and vinegar into a blender and blend till smooth. With the motor running, open the hatch in the blender lid and trickle in the vegetable oil to form an emulsion. Add as much oil as necessary till the mixture becomes so thick that it no longer spins inside the blender. At that stage, add in the lemon juice and blend till the mixture no longer spins inside the blender again. Adjust to taste with salt and more vinegar if necessary.

To make the pickled garlic, combine all the ingredients in a bowl and allow to sit for at least 2 hours.

When ready to serve, heat a little olive oil in a frying pan over high heat. Once the oil starts to smoke, add the broccoli in a single layer. Allow it to pan-roast without tossing or turning. Season well with salt and pepper. When the broccoli has developed charred brown edges, turn the pieces over and allow to char on the other side. Add the chilli slices into the pan along with the butter and toss well. Allow to cook for 1 minute more and transfer to a large bowl. Spoon 3 tablespoons of the anchovy sauce and the pickled garlic over the broccoli. Toss to combine and place on a serving platter. Garnish with a few more pickled garlic slices.

AVOCADO SMOOTHIE

½ avocado
1 cup cold water,
    plus additional for adjusting
1 tbsp lime juice
¼ cup extra virgin olive oil
Salt

NUOC CHAM

½ cup fish sauce
½ cup rice wine vinegar
½ cup white sugar
½ cup water
1 clove garlic, smashed
1 red chilli
    (or more if you like), chopped
4 fresh coriander stems, chopped

Vegetable oil, for deep-frying
300 g baby corn
1 handful fresh mint, roughly torn
1 large shallot, thinly sliced into rings

FRIED BABY CORN

WITH AVOCADO SMOOTHIE, NUOC CHAM AND MINT

On our company trip to Vietnam in early 2014, we hit the streets and gorged ourselves on a ton of amazing things. One that stood out for me (and that I had every day I was there), was the avocado smoothie. Sweet, creamy, thick and deliciously vegetal—I'd never tasted avocado like that before. I wanted to recreate it as a savoury dish back at Artichoke. It became the base for a dish of fried baby corn, tossed in nuoc cham for that distinctive Vietnamese flavour.

»»»»»

To make the avocado smoothie, place the avocado and the cold water in a blender and blend till you get a smooth, runny consistency—like a regular smoothie. Note that all avocados are different; some might require a little more than 1 cup of water to liquefy. Don't be afraid to pour in additional water if necessary. With the motor running, open the hatch in the blender and add the lime juice. Trickle in the olive oil bit by bit till everything is incorporated. Season well with salt. Keep chilled.

To make the nuoc cham, mix all the ingredients together and allow to sit for at least 30 minutes to allow the flavours to develop.

Preheat the oil in a deep fryer to 180°C. If you don't have a deep fryer, heat 10cm of vegetable oil in a deep pot or saucepan over high heat till it reaches 180°C. When the oil is hot enough, deep-fry the whole ears of baby corn for 2 to 3 minutes till they are deep brown on the outside. Toss them in a bowl with the nuoc cham, mint and shallot rings. Place the avocado smoothie on the bottom of a deep plate and top with a mound of the nouc cham-dressed baby corn.

SERVES 4

CHERMOULA

4 large tomatoes, chopped
1 large red onion, chopped
4 large red chillis,
 seeds removed and chopped
10 g ginger, peeled and chopped
8 cloves garlic
2 tsp cumin powder
2 tsp coriander powder
1 tsp turmeric powder
2 tbsp salt
1 tbsp black pepper
75 ml olive oil
1 tbsp lemon juice

CHERMOULA ONION RELISH

2 tbsp olive oil
1 large red onion, thinly sliced
5 tbsp chermoula
60 g pitted green olives,
 roughly chopped
Salt and pepper

PRESERVED LEMON BUTTER

150 g unsalted butter, softened
Rind of ¼ a preserved lemon*,
 finely chopped

1 whole fish (400 to 600 g),
 scaled and gutted, or 400 to
 600 g fish fillets/steaks**
1 lemon, halved
Fresh herbs (such as baby coriander
 or celery cress), for garnish (optional)

CHERMOULA BBQ FISH
WITH PRESERVED LEMON BUTTER

In Vietnam, we saw tons of open pit BBQs by the roadside, grilling all manner of seafood: prawns, fish, clams and shells. The smells and flavours were incredible; I wanted to recreate them at Artichoke. We came back and dreamt up a Moroccan-inspired grilled fish, rubbed with chermoula (a herby, spicy, fresh wet marinade for meats and fish) and smeared with tart, fragrant preserved lemon butter. On top of that, we created a chermoula onion relish, both as an excuse to spam more of the seasoning on as well as add another layer of sweetness to the dish. This recipe yields about 3 cups of chermoula paste, which can keep for 1 to 2 days tops in the fridge.

》》》》》

To make the chermoula, throw everything together in a food processor and blend till smooth. The result should resemble a salsa —chunky, yet slightly watery.

To make the onion relish, heat the olive oil in a non-stick frying pan over medium heat. Fry the onion slices for 4 minutes, or until they begin to soften and caramelise. Add in the chermoula and cook for a further 3 to 4 minutes, until the paste darkens and the onions are fairly soft. Remove from the heat and fold in the chopped olives. Season well with salt and pepper and allow to cool. **》**

*Preserved lemons are pickled in a brine of salt, water and their own juices. They're common in Moroccan cuisine, and the rinds are prized for the concentrated dose of lemony zing when added to stews, marinades, or salad dressings. You'll be able to find them at gourmet grocers.

**If using a whole fish, I'd recommend sea bass, pomfret, mackerel and baby snapper. If you're going for fillets, there are more options to pick from. Cod, red snapper and Spanish mackerel are great, but you can also ball out with tuna and salmon steaks too.

To make the preserved lemon butter, beat the butter and the lemon rind in a bowl. You can make this a couple of days early; it stores pretty well. Just remember to bring it to room temperature 30 minutes before use, so that it spreads easily.

Preheat a charcoal grill. Make 2 to 3 deep scores down the sides of the fish with a sharp knife, running them from the top fins right down to the bottom fins. Rub in as much chermoula as the fish will hold. Don't worry about rubbing in too much because the excess will drip off anyway. If using fillets, just rub the chermoula right on. Let the fish sit for at least 20 minutes in the paste.

Grill the fish over charcoal till it is cooked through, flipping it over a couple of times to cook both sides. The time it takes to cook depends on factors such as the size and thickness of the fish, the heat of the coals, the distance between the coals and the fish, etc. I can't really give you an exact cooking time, but a ballpark figure for cooking over a medium flame would be 10 to 15 minutes in total. However, I can tell you how to check that it's cooked: poke a metal skewer or a paring knife into the thickest part of the flesh. Remove it and place it on the fattest part of your palm, just below your thumb. If the skewer tip feels hot, the fish is cooked. If it feels just warm-ish, let the fish cook a while longer till a second try yields a hot skewer.

While the fish is cooking, place the lemon halves cut side down onto the cooking grates. What you're after are lemon halves that are nicely charred and really warm and juicy when you squeeze them later. Charring the lemon kinda makes its juice a little sweeter and less acidic.

Transfer the fish to a plate. If you want to be fancy, you can trim off any burnt fins/tails with a pair of kitchen scissors. Smear the fish heavily with 1 to 2 tablespoons of preserved lemon butter at room temperature. Top with a couple of heaped spoonfuls of the onion relish and the herbs. Squeeze juice from the charred lemons over the whole thing and attack.

CHAPTER 17

Lolly Bags

>>>>>

Since day one, we've been giving out bags of gummy bears to our guests when they leave after a meal. Apart from the fact that I survived on sour gummies as a university student abroad, this has almost zero relevance to the food that we serve. However, it does make people smile on their way out and concludes their experience on a positive note.

Food that's real, messy, flavour-focused and full of down-home, Ginuwine-level soul.

It's always heartening to see people leave happy.

Growing up, what made me happy was Boyz II Men. (I remember sending an envelope stuffed with money and an application to their Fan Club headquarters in the US.) When my buddies were playing soccer, I dabbled in basketball. When Leon Lai was in vogue, I was vibing to Luther Vandross. You can probably guess by now (if you haven't already) that my favourite foods orbited the sphere of fried chicken, watermelon and anything gravy-soaked. Food that's not necessarily prepared with technical wizardry. Food that's real, messy, flavour-focused and full of down-home, Ginuwine-level soul.

I believe this quality is something you can't recreate in your food without the right heart. You can design a sleek-ass restaurant and create a smart, funky menu, but if you don't have soul to begin with, nothing you try to do will be able to compensate.

So at Artichoke, we start with food that makes us happy. Hence the improbable creations like Oreo 'Pancakes' (page 234) and Ridiculous Cookie Cakes (page 237). Hence the sharing plates and communal menu, to get you guys engaging with each other during your meal. One of my favourite eating experiences is delivered by Cajun Kings (shout out!), where various crustaceans are chucked unto the table and whenever you smash down hard on a crab claw, it shoots into your partner's eye. It brings everyone closer together.

These posters are not strictly necessary. But they make us happy, therefore they exist.

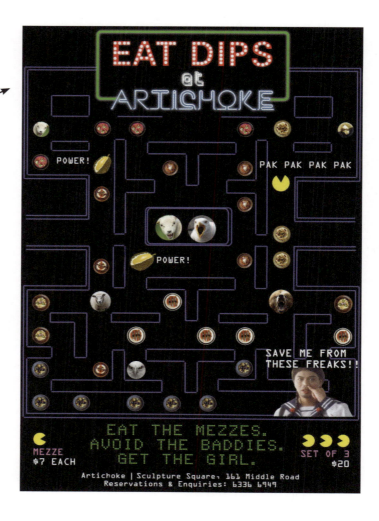

The bottom line is—we don't cook for our egos; we don't cook to display our technical prowess (because we have none). Some restaurants turn out theatrical compositions, piled neck-high and adorned with foams and gels. "Look what we can do!" they scream. Here, though, the subtext is a little more like "Hey, I'm sure you'll be happy with a big-ass plate of fried chicken that you could never finish", appended with a smiley face.

We are, essentially, in the business of making people feel happy. With that in mind, here are some recipes to make you feel good about spending $50 on this book. Sometimes, they don't make much sense. Who cares? Borat didn't make any sense whatsoever, but is still my favourite feel-good movie of all time.

Very naisssseeee.....

SMOKING IT UP EVERYDAY
OUR NEWEST TOY: CHINESE DRUM SMOKER
Habitos Tambor Chino!
LOAD UP THIS BAD BOY WITH A BUNCH OF BIRDS, SET ITS ASS ON FIRE
=
Smoked Chicken, Lebanese Pickles, Garden Herb Relish, Toum Garlic Whip
TWENTY SIX BUCKS
AND NO, WE DID NOT CAUSE THE HAZE. TQVM.
Artichoke | Sculpture Square, 161 Middle Road
Reservations & Enquiries: 6336 6949

MAKES
1
SANDWICH

HARISSA-SPICED CRAB PATE

100 g unsalted butter

5 shallots, finely chopped

250 g crabmeat (freshly picked
   or the good quality canned variety)

40 g Japanese mayonnaise
   (Kewpie brand)

About 10 stalks chives, finely chopped

½ tbsp lemon juice

1 or more tbsp nori harissa (page 231)

Salt and pepper

1 to 2 tbsp unsalted butter

2 slices good quality sourdough
   or ciabatta

3 fillets pickled anchovies
   (also popularly known as
   'boquerones en vinagre',
   in Spanish)

1 piece roasted sweet pepper,
   from a jar

1 small handful rocket

Saffron Mayo, to serve
   (page 255, optional)

C.R.A.P SANDWICH

At one point in time, we were testing out the theory of reverse psychology on our unsuspecting brunch customers. We'd put dishes on our menu with out-there names like Suicide, Atomic Bomb, Self-Destruction and the C.R.A.P Sandwich. The description of the dish would be followed by a disclaimer: 'If you're smart, do not order this'. Then we'd just hide behind a pillar and watch as customers perused the menu. Usually they'd laugh. A surprising number of them would order the dish and have fun doing it. And the best part was—if they didn't like it, they'd blame themselves. (I think I might have just hit upon the secret recipe for success.) Anyway, it's all in good fun. This recipe is, obviously, not crap at all; the acronym stands for Crab pate, Rocket, Anchovies and Peppers.

This recipe yields about 1½ cups of crab pate. It will keep for 2 days in the fridge. When not eating in a sandwich, you may serve this as a starter, along with warm flatbread and a good amount of pickles (page 257) to balance out the richness.

》》》》》

To make the crab pate, heat the butter over low heat in a frying pan. Add the shallots and sweat for 5 minutes. Allow to cool to room temperature. Place the shallot butter in a mixing bowl with all the pate ingredients and mix well. Season to taste with salt and pepper, and throw in more nori harissa if you like. Transfer the pate into a Mason jar or ramekin and chill for at least 4 hours.

To assemble the sandwich, melt the butter in a frying pan over medium-high heat. Toast the bread slices in the butter till golden and crispy on both sides. Spread 2 tablespoons of crab pate onto one slice of bread and top with the anchovy fillets, roasted pepper and rocket. Drizzle with the mayo, then complete the sandwich with the other slice of bread. Eat quickly while the bread is hot and the contents are cold.

Pinch of salt
20 quail eggs, at room temperature
½ litre ice water
1 tbsp vinegar
    (preferably a light variety,
    such as rice, white wine or
    cider vinegar)
Cumin salt, to serve*

*To make the cumin salt, mix
1 part crushed, toasted cumin
seeds to 3 parts crushed sea salt.

SOFT-BOILED QUAIL EGGS
WITH CUMIN SALT

Quail eggs have always been a nostalgic dish for me. My mom would make me quail eggs as a teatime snack when I was a child. I would take a long time to crack them open, but it was always worth it. On the company trip to Vietnam earlier in 2014, we stumbled across this vendor selling quail eggs that were dipped into chilli salt before eating. The salt brought out the flavour of the eggs well, so for an Artichoke-d version, I concocted a cumin salt instead.

»»»»

Bring water to a boil in a pot and add a pinch of salt. Place the quail eggs gently into the water and boil for exactly 1 minute 45 seconds (use a kitchen timer). Transfer the eggs gently to a bowl containing a mixture of ice water and the vinegar for at least 10 minutes. The vinegar in the ice bath helps the egg shells come off easily. Peel the eggs and allow them to revert back to room temperature. Serve with cumin salt for dipping.

My mom would make me quail eggs as a teatime snack when I was a child.

4

TAHINI LEMON DRESSING

3 tbsp tahini
1 tbsp lemon juice
1 clove garlic, finely chopped
1 tsp pomegranate molasses
1 tbsp white sesame seeds, toasted
1 tbsp soy sauce
Water, to adjust
Salt and pepper

1 red onion, quartered
1 tsp clear honey
1 tbsp red wine vinegar
1 tbsp olive oil
1 sprig thyme
Salt and pepper
½ zucchini
¼ cup pistachios
1 cup roasting juice reserved
   from lamb roast (page 119),
   plus additional for warming
   the lamb shoulder
200 g roast lamb shoulder (page 119)
4 generous handfuls mixed
   salad leaves (such as raddichio,
   romaine, oak lettuce, watercress
   or rocket)
Lemon juice, to garnish
Extra virgin olive oil, for drizzling

LAMB SHOULDER SALAD
WITH TAHINI LEMON DRESSING AND BRAISED PISTACHIOS

This is one of those dishes that isn't at all healthy, but makes you feel otherwise. That's why I've lumped it under the 'Feel Good' recipe umbrella. This salad is also a great way to use up any leftover Lambgasm (page 119).

》》》》

To make the tahini lemon dressing, combine all the ingredients, except the water, in a bowl. Whisk in water gradually, till the mixture just starts to become runny, sort of like an oil-based paint. Season to taste with salt and pepper.

Preheat your oven to 180°C. Place the onion quarters onto a sheet of aluminum foil and drizzle with the honey, vinegar and olive oil. Add the thyme and season well with salt and pepper, then wrap the foil up into a closed 'pouch'. Roast the onions for 45 minutes. Tear the 'pouch' open and roast for a further 10 minutes to brown the onions. At this point, the onions should fall apart easily into layers and boast a nice, roasted sweetness.

While the onions are roasting, shave the zucchini into long, thin ribbons with a vegetable peeler. Set aside. Simmer the pistachios with the lamb roasting juice for 15 minutes, adding more water along the way if the sauce starts to dry up. You should end up with pistachios that are plump and tender, and a sauce thick enough to glaze the back of a metal spoon. Season to taste with more salt and pepper, if necessary. Set aside.

Just before serving, warm the lamb in more of its roasting juices in a saucepan. Just a low simmer will do; there's no need to bring to a boil. Shred the lamb roughly with your fingers or a couple of forks. Place in a large mixing bowl along with the roast onions, braised pistachios and the reduced pistachio-lamb sauce, zucchini ribbons, roasting juice and the salad leaves. Dress with just enough tahini lemon dressing to coat the leaves, and season again with salt and pepper, if necessary. Drizzle with more lemon juice and extra virgin olive oil if that's what floats your boat.

NORI HARISSA

4 large sheets nori
5 large dried chillies
10 cloves garlic
2 small shallots
2 tbsp cumin powder
1 tbsp clear honey
2 tbsp lemon juice
1 cup water,
    plus additional for adjusting
6 tbsp olive oil
Sea salt

8 chicken wings
Vegetable oil, for deep-frying
1 cup rice flour or corn flour
2 tbsp unsalted butter, melted
Sea salt
1 small handful fresh coriander
Lime wedges

FRIED CHICKEN WINGS
WITH NORI HARISSA

Chicken wings are always a failsafe feel-good dish, and so are seaweed chicken nuggets (a fatty nugget encircled by a thin slice of seaweed, commonly found at pasar malams, or local night markets). So we decided to combine the two by tossing chicken wings in a harissa dressing spiked with nori (Japanese seaweed). Harissa is a fiery North African chilli relish, somewhat similar to a South East Asian sambal. The addition of nori adds a depth of flavour (i.e. umami) that kicks this already awesome relish up to a whole new level. The harissa will keep as long as 1 week in the fridge. You can use it in dishes like the Tuna 'Kibbeh Nayeh' (page 91), Tuna Tartare with Pork Crackling (page 169) and the C.R.A.P Sandwich (page 227).

»»»»

To make the nori harissa, soak the nori sheets in water for 5 minutes then remove and squeeze dry. Place all the ingredients, apart from the nori and salt, into a blender and blitz everything into a smoothie. Heat a non-stick frying pan over low heat. Tip the contents of the blender into the pan and stir constantly to prevent the bottom of the mix from burning. After 8 to 10 minutes, the mixture will become a thick, dark red, extremely fragrant paste. Transfer it back into the blender and leave to cool. Add the soaked nori and blend once more. Add more water to loosen the paste if it's too dry. Adjust to taste with more lemon juice, honey or salt.

Marinate the wings with 2 tablespoons of nori harissa for at least an hour. Ideally, you'll let it marinate overnight. Preheat the oil in a deep fryer to 180°C. If you don't have a deep fryer, heat 10cm of vegetable oil in a deep pot or saucepan over high heat till it reaches 180°C. Coat the wings in the rice flour. Shake off excess flour and once the oil is hot enough, deep-fry for 4 to 6 minutes, till the wings are cooked through. Place in a large mixing bowl with the butter and 4 tablespoons of nori harissa. Season to taste with sea salt and toss well. Plate up the glazed wings along with some coriander leaves and lime wedges.

ROSEWATER SYRUP
1 part water
1 part sugar
A few drops rosewater (page 17)

1 watermelon

ROSE + WATER + MELON

Our riff on the vodka watermelon. Instead of injecting the unsuspecting fruit with a shit-ton of alcohol, we're making this slightly more PG by using rosewater.

〉〉〉〉〉

To make the syrup, bring the water and sugar to a boil in a deep pot or saucepan. Reserve about 500 ml of syrup and add in a few drops of rosewater. Mix well.

Use a knife to cut out a small hole (about 0.5cm in diameter) in the watermelon. Stick a funnel into the hole and pour the reserved syrup in slowly until it's absorbed. Alternatively, you may use a large syringe (pictured) to inject the bugger. When the melon can't absorb any more liquid, stick it into the fridge. The longer you chill it, the more time the rosewater has to distribute itself through the fruit. I recommend at least 6 hours. When ready to eat, slice the melon up generously and slurp away.

OREO 'PANCAKES'

1 box instant pancake mix
As many Oreos as necessary
  to use up the batter
Unsalted butter, for frying

Serve the 'pancakes' with kiddy
stuff like ice cream, maple
syrup, chocolate sauce, crushed
nuts, etc. We like to add pureed
beetroot into the pancake mix
so that the final product is a
sorta-red velvet pancake.

When you knock off at 11.30pm every night and reach home
at midnight, there's not much social activity left to join in. So I
spend a lot of my time on mind-disintegrating websites, looking
at random stuff like muffins that resemble sheep and pancake-
coated Kit Kats. I thought, shit, I should do this with Oreos. (I
love Oreos.) So I cribbed some of Overdoughs' stash—namely
Oreos and pancake mix—the next day and tried it out. The
results? Awesome. The cookies steam inside the moisture from the
heated pancake batter and soften up; the final result resembles a
chocolate cake with a layer of vanilla cream.

»»»»»

For this super simple recipe, make the pancake batter by following
the instructions on the packet. Dunk the Oreos into the batter.
Grease the bottom of a non-stick frying pan with the butter,
then fry the pancakes over medium heat.

Alternatively, the recipe also works wonders with things like Kit Kats and Snickers bars; basically anything that pancake batter can cling to and that goes squishy when heated.

Cakes can be themed however you like it; they are the vehicles for your unbounded creativity. Here are some cake-topping ideas to get you started: Breakfast (cereal, bananas, nuts, pancake bits), Frat House (crushed ramen bits, bacon bits, bourbon, pizza, chicken nuggets), At The Movies (cola gummies, popcorn, chocolate bars, Doritos), Snickers (chocolate, peanuts, salted caramel, nougat), Singaporean Drinks (bandung-flavoured icing, aloe vera, tapioca pearls, Horlicks candy).

COOKIE DOUGH

2 cups unsalted butter,
   at room temperature
2 cups white sugar
2 cups brown sugar
4 eggs
2 tsp vanilla bean paste
4 tsp orange blossom water (page 17)
2 tsp cinnamon powder
2 tsp baking soda
4 tsp hot water
1 tsp salt
6 cups plain flour
3 cups dark chocolate buttons
½ cup Turkish delight,
   roughly chopped (optional)
2 cups flaked almonds

ROSE CREAM

2 kg cream cheese
500 g icing sugar
3 tsp rosewater

TOPPINGS—ANY COMBINATION OF THE FOLLOWING

Strawberries, raspberries, bananas,
   dried fruit, candy bars, gummy
   bears, marshmallows, cotton candy,
   breakfast cereal, popcorn, nuts,
   maple syrup, bacon bits, meringue...
   the list goes on.

RIDICULOUS COOKIE CAKE

At one point in time, mega-high, towering cakes were all the rage. We wanted to do our own version of that, and came up with this ridiculous number. (It was so well received we've even served it at a couple of weddings.) The cookies should be baked till not totally soft, yet not totally crispy either. They're layered atop each other with a layer of frosting in between and a smattering of crazy toppings. The best way to eat this dessert would be to slice into it as you would a normal cake.

»»»»

To make the cookie dough, put the butter, white sugar and brown sugar in the bowl of an electric mixer and beat until smooth and pale. Using the electric mixer, beat in the eggs one at a time. Stir in the vanilla paste, orange blossom water and cinnamon. Dissolve the baking soda in the water and add to the mixture, then throw in the salt. Fold in the flour and remaining cookie dough ingredients by hand till well incorporated. Line 3 quarter sheet pans (about 33cm by 23cm) with greaseproof paper. Divide the dough evenly over the pans in scoops, using a large spoon or an ice cream scoop. Make sure the dough lumps are spaced about one ball apart; you want them to melt and flatten to form an intact sheet as they bake. Refrigerate for at least 2 hours.

When ready to bake, preheat your oven to 180°C and bake for 15 minutes, or until the dough is brown around the edges. Leave to cool.

To make the rose cream, beat the cream cheese in the bowl of an electric mixer till it becomes soft and spreadable. Add in the icing sugar one spoonful at a time till all the sugar has been incorporated. Beat in the rosewater. Chill in the fridge for at least 2 hours.

To assemble, gently remove the cookie sheets from the sheet pans and peel off the greaseproof paper. Place the first layer of cookie on a serving platter and spread ⅓ of the rose cream over it. Place a second cookie sheet over and repeat till you end up with a final layer of cream at the top. Decorate the top of the 'cake' with the toppings of your choice.

EAT
JOYFULLY

SERVES 4

BASE INGREDIENTS

1 part whipped cream
(while you can use store-bought
cream-from-the-can, freshly whipped
cream is always superior*)

1 part store-bought meringue,
coarsely crushed

MASH-INS (ANY COMBINATION AND AMOUNT YOU LIKE)

Popping boba (those juice-filled
pearls you find in bubble tea
that burst in the mouth)

Fruit-flavoured Jell-O

Any fruit jam

Any poached fruit (such as
apricots, pears, peaches, etc.)

Fresh fruit (such as strawberries,
banana, plums, etc.)

Broken candy bars (such as
Twix, Crunch, Crunchie, etc.)

Chocolate sauce

Caramel sauce

Toasted nuts

Marshmallows

Ice cream

Peanut butter

Nutella

Marshmallow fluff

Dulce de leche

Fudge chunks

Brownie chunks

Cookie chunks

Nougat chunks

Breakfast cereal

DESSERT SMASH-UP

So. We started with the idea of an Eton Mess, with its core crew of cream, meringue and dried, cooked or fresh fruit. And tarted it up beyond recognition. In line with the fact that we tend to take things a little too far, we folded in influences from ice kachang and halo-halo (a Philippine iced snack) to add texture: popping pearls, Jell-O, crushed peanuts... the list goes on. This is not strictly a recipe, but an idea you can pick up and run with. Just throw whatever you like together with reckless abandon!

»»»»

Place the whipped cream and meringue into a large mixing bowl. Add in any other mash-ins that you have on hand. Mix everything up. Pile high in a bowl. Garnish with more toppings if you want.

*HOW TO WHIP YOUR OWN CREAM

There's no such thing as low fat whipped cream. Use either whipping cream or heavy cream, both of which have a milkfat content of at least 30 per cent. Cream doubles in size after whipping—1 cup of whipping cream makes about 2 cups. It's important to whip the cream when it's chilled; on a hot day, you might want to chill your whisk and bowl too. Using a stand mixer, hand mixer or good ol' hands and whisk, whip away. If using an electric mixer, keep the speed between medium and medium-high. Whip for about 7 to 9 minutes, until the cream starts to form soft peaks. For that Artichoke touch, add in a couple of drops of orange blossom water or rosewater before whipping.

CHAPTER 18

Overdoughs

》》》》》

Two years into Artichoke, Overdoughs was born. She's the love child of Roxanne (yeah, the one who complained about the beetroot salad) and me, but her early days weren't exactly smooth.

We found a little shop space on the ground floor of Waterloo Centre, just across the road from Artichoke. It seemed like the perfect spot—just a hop, skip and jump away from the mothership, and with just enough room to house a small breakaway team focused on making sweet things.

In her first two months, Overdoughs did well. The idea was to extend Artichoke's philosophy into the dessert realm, with the same schizoid split between Middle Eastern influences and all-out barely sane creations. A small band of loyal customers started to trickle in from nearby offices and schools to fill up the 16-seat communal table in the afternoons, fuelling up on baklavas, Snickers tarts, pomegranate chocolate cakes, bacon sticky buns, mint teas and Turkish sodas. Everything was sweet (no pun intended).

Then one afternoon, the letter came. The government was telling us that the plot of land right in front of the bakery was going to be converted into the China Cultural Centre, and that construction would commence the following month. How bad could it be, we thought. So we hung back and waited.

BOOM. Every afternoon, the ruckus of piling was unbearable. The contractors erected a storey-high scaffolding just across the 2m-wide walkway from Overdoughs' doorstep, shielding it from the **construction**. But it didn't do much to block off the noise and mini-earthquakes that went on for weeks.

Our baby's 16 seats were now empty. In fact, every shop along the same stretch was pretty much empty too. Loyal customers would still come for their weekly fix, but it was more a grab-and-

Overdoughs, according to my exact specifications, was designed 'to look like an illegal, guerrilla-style pop-up. None of that twee, cosy shit.'

run affair. Just as quickly as business picked up when we opened, it was now halving by the week.

We made the tough decision to cut our losses. Construction was set to go on for two years, and these guys weren't exactly knitting sweaters over there. We had to leave.

So we packed up, broke our lease and forfeited the one-month rent deposit as an early termination penalty. Fortunately, the entire interior of Overdoughs, according to my exact specifications, was designed 'to look like an illegal, guerrilla-style pop-up. None of that

twee, cosy shit'. We were back safe in the mothership within a couple of days.

Losing the entire six-figure sum we'd sunk into acquiring the Overdoughs space, renovating it, then spending barely four months there was rough. It was like a Muay Thai kick to the groin. But looking back at the financials, it was a good move, and I'm glad we did it. If we had stayed on for a couple more months, we'd have bled to death. Overdoughs had narrowly escaped total closure.

One year on, the bakery still operates next to Artichoke. Though there's no longer enough space to bake bread every day like we used to, we like how this arrangement is working out. It's nicer when we're closer to each other, literally side-by-side. On the back end, the boys and girls of both entities can lend each other a hand whenever one's needed, and they get to prank each other more often (page 260). On the front end, customers can simply pop over to Overdoughs after their meal for sugary treats that make them smile.

Sweet endings all around.

OVERDOUGHS

SALTED DULCE DE LECHE

1 small can (400 ml) condensed milk
Generous pinch of sea salt

MUFFIN BATTER

5 bananas (preferably very ripe ones)
2 large eggs
70 g unsalted butter, melted
240 g cake flour
5 g baking soda
5 g baking powder
¼ tsp salt
150 g caster sugar
50 g fresh blueberries

MARSHMALLOW CRUMBLE

60 g plain flour
20 g caster sugar
40 g unsalted butter, melted
30 g mini marshmallows

BANANA BLUEBERRY MUFFIN
WITH MARSHMALLOW CRUMBLE AND SALTED DULCE DE LECHE

Kel, sick bastard and head baker at Overdoughs, came up with this monster. He took the humble banana muffin and pumped it up with blueberries, marshmallows and dulce de leche. It looks totally alien and fugly, but that's the point of this muffin. He also likes to make his muffins look extra hardcore, so he garnishes the top with even more things like crispy banana chips or pretzel bits. You can go balls out and do the same for yours if you like.

»»»»

To make the dulce de leche, boil the unopened can of condensed milk in a pot full of water for 4 hours. Make sure the can is completely submerged. Check on it every hour or so to make sure that the water does not dry up. Top up with more water if necessary. Water regulates the temperature of the can. If the water dries up and the can is allowed to get red-hot, it will explode, leaving everyone in the room with nasty-ass burns. So exercise some caution here. After 4 hours, leave the can of condensed milk to cool completely, before opening it. The contents should have turned dark gold in colour. Stir in the sea salt.

To make the muffin batter, mash 3 bananas well and mix with the eggs and butter. Fold in the cake flour, baking soda, baking powder, salt and caster sugar. Chop up the last two bananas and fold into the batter along with the blueberries. Set aside.

To make the crumble, mix the plain flour, sugar and butter in a bowl. Fold in the marshmallows.

Preheat your oven to 170°C. Grease a 6-in-1 muffin tray and spoon in enough muffin batter to come ⅔ of the way up the sides. Scatter the marshmallow crumble over the batter and bake for 30 minutes. Remove from the oven and immediately douse the muffin tops with the salted dulce de leche.

SYRUP
500 g sugar
500 ml water
4 tbsp clear honey
½ tsp orange blossom water (page 17)
½ tsp rosewater

250 g clarified butter,
   plus additional in case
   you want to spam on
   the butter, melted
12 sheets filo pastry
Nut filling*

BAKLAVA

This is a more or less classic recipe—Overdoughs is a Middle Eastern-associated bakery, after all. While I have no issue with the traditional version, here are a couple of slightly left-of-centre variations—3-nut, bacon nut and chocolate almond baklava. The pastry keeps well for 1 to 2 weeks at room temperature because the butter and sugar act as preservatives. If you're planning to diet-ify this recipe by using less butter and sugar, that's cool with me. You already paid for this book anyway, so you deserve the right to change things (unless you shoplifted it, you thieving SOB). But back to my point: be aware that its shelf life will decrease significantly if you use less sugar and/or butter.

»»»»

To make the syrup, bring the sugar, water and honey to a boil, then simmer for 5 minutes. Allow to cool for 5 minutes before adding the orange blossom water and rosewater.

Preheat your oven to 160°C. Grease a quarter sheet baking pan (about 23 by 33cm) with some of the butter. Lay four sheets of filo over each other in the pan, brushing each layer with more butter after it is laid down. Sprinkle half of your nut filling over. Lay another four sheets of filo over the nuts, again brushing each sheet with butter. Sprinkle the remaining nut filling over, and top with the final four sheets of filo. Cut through the pastry with a small sharp knife into your desired shape (rectangles, squares, diamonds, etc.). Run your knife down these cuts twice to make sure that the pastry is cut all the way down to the bottom. Pour extra butter over these cuts. You may or may not use up all your butter, depending on how heavily you've brushed your filo sheets previously. Just know that more butter helps to make your baklavas more delicious and less dry.

Bake the baklava for 80 minutes. While it is still hot, pour over enough syrup to saturate the layers. You'll know they are saturated when you can see the syrup rise up between the cracks. Now, resist the temptation to eat it straight away. Wait for the baklava to cool down and absorb all that sugar syrup before tucking in. It's worth the wait, trust me.

*3-NUT FILLING

115 g walnuts
115 g pistachios
400 g almonds
150 g caster sugar
3 tsp orange blossom water

Blitz all the ingredients in a food processor.

BACON AND NUT FILLING

Add 100 g of cooked crispy bacon to the 3-nut filling before blitzing in a food processor. If you're heading down this route, add the rendered bacon fat to the clarified butter, and consider swapping the honey in the syrup for 6 tbsp of maple syrup.

CHOCOLATE ALMOND FILLING

650 g almonds
2 tsp cinnamon powder
150 g caster sugar
150 g semi-sweet
   chocolate chips

Blitz all the ingredients in a food processor.

EAT SWEETLY

250 g white chocolate buttons

BASIC COOKIE DOUGH
400 g unsalted butter, softened
285 g caster sugar
185 g brown sugar
3 eggs
1 tsp vanilla paste
Pinch of salt
400 g self-raising flour
200 g wasabi peas
150 g dried cranberries

WASABI PEA AND

CARAMELISED WHITE CHOCOLATE COOKIES

One day in the kitchen, we burnt some white chocolate by accident. But we found that it tasted great. (Kinda like Fleming and penicillin, with decidedly tastier results.) When burnt white chocolate cools, it tastes like a crispy, caramel-chocolatey honeycomb. I'd describe it as the 'inside of a Violet Crumble'. The combination of white chocolate and wasabi is not common, but not unheard of: the sweet creaminess of chocolate is set off by the delicate heat of a pinch of wasabi. Of course, at Artichoke and Overdoughs we take things one rung lower on the ladder of culinary classiness, and use wasabi peas instead.

»»»»

To make the caramelised white chocolate, heat up a non-stick frying pan and melt the white chocolate buttons over medium-high heat. As the mixture bubbles, it will start to darken in colour around the edges. Turn down the heat and stir the brown edges into the middle and let new brown edges form. Keep cooking till the whole mixture turns a light brown, like latte. Pour out onto a tray lined with greaseproof paper or a silicone sheet. Leave to cool and set. Break up the caramelised chocolate into small, 1cm-sized bits. Try a piece. If you think it tastes amazing (like I do), say bye to the rest of the recipe and just go munch on these right now.

If you have enough determination to carry on, then make the cookie dough. Cream the butter, caster sugar and brown sugar in the bowl of an electric mixer for about 2 minutes on medium-high speed, or until the mixture is fluffy and light. With the mixer running, add in the eggs one at a time, each one in fully before adding the next. Add the vanilla paste, salt and flour and beat on low speed till the mixture just comes together. Do not overwork it or your cookies might come out tough. Throw in the wasabi peas, dried cranberries and caramelised white chocolate bits, and mix again with the electric mixer on medium speed till just combined. Transfer the batter to a container and let it chill in the fridge for at least an hour.

When ready to bake, preheat your oven to 170°C. Use an ice cream scoop to get uniform-sized balls of dough out of the container.

Line a baking tray with greaseproof paper (or use a silicone sheet), and place these balls of dough at least two spaces apart from each other. If the dough balls are around the size of a golf ball, or slightly larger, bake them anywhere from 10 to 15 minutes.

The baking time will ultimately depend on the size of the balls, and how soft or crisp you like your cookies. If you like your cookies semi-soft like I do, pull them out at 10 to 12 minutes in and eat them while they're still warm. The best way to gauge the time is to look at the colour. Cookies start to brown from the edges in. If you like your cookies really squishy, take them out when the brown edges come just 30 per cent in. If you want them semi-soft, remove them at the 60 per cent mark. Let them brown fully if you enjoy super crispy cookies.

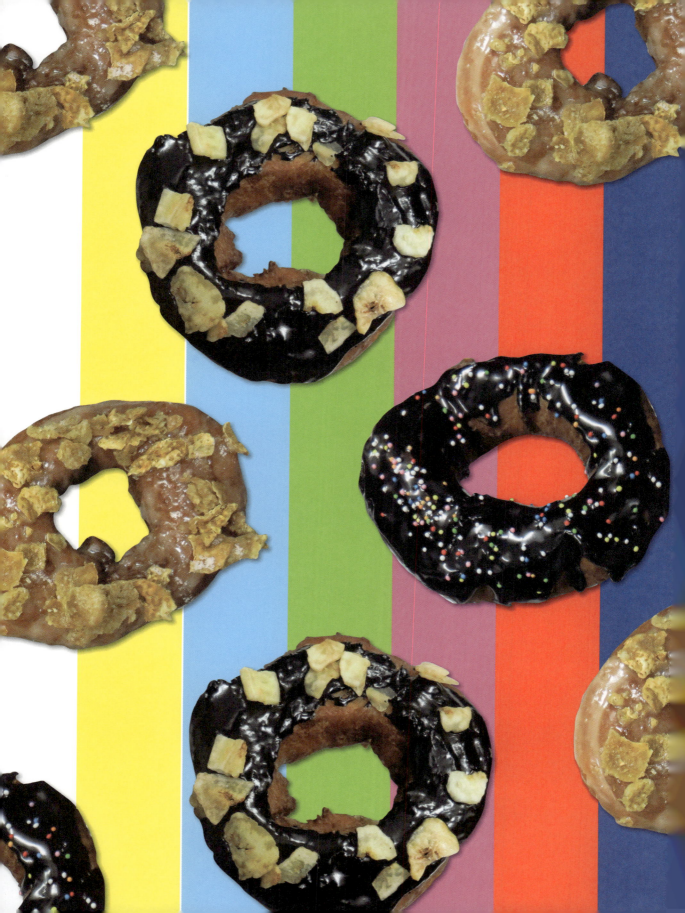

DONUTS

50 g sugar
7 g dry yeast
50 ml water, lukewarm
70 ml milk, lukewarm
1 egg
15 g unsalted butter, melted
5 g salt
250 g all-purpose flour,
    plus additional for sprinkling
Vegetable oil, for deep-frying
Coarse white sugar

SALTED MAPLE GLAZE

4 tbsp unsalted butter, melted
1 cup icing sugar
8 tbsp maple syrup
½ tsp smoked sea salt

SOME IDEAS FOR TOPPINGS

Popcorn
Chocolate chips
Butterscotch chips
Broken candy bars
Freeze-dried berries
Banana chips
Pop Rocks
Chicken or pork skin crackling
Nerds (the candy, not the humans)
Skittles
Candied bacon bits
Crushed tortilla chips
Crushed potato crisps
Pickles
Crushed Oreos
Jalapenos
Shredded cheese
Gummy bears
Beer nuts
Breakfast cereal

DONUTS
OF YOUR WILDEST IMAGINATION

When we say 'wildest imagination', we mean it. Be the master of your own donuts. Wanna stud the maple glaze with pork cracklings? Do it. How about smoked paprika powder and Pop Rocks, or salted chocolate and chicken skin? No one's saying no. Don't sit on your ass and fantasize—make it happen.

»»»»

To make the donuts, throw the sugar, yeast, water, milk, egg and butter into the mixing bowl of a dough mixer. Mix on low speed and allow to sit for 10 minutes till froth starts to form at the top. Add in the salt and flour and beat using the dough hook attachment for 5 minutes till the dough is smooth and elastic. Rest the dough for 1 hour at room temperature, wrapped in lightly greased cling film.

Sprinkle some flour onto a flat surface and roll out the dough into a flat sheet that's roughly 2cm thick. Using a large, round cookie-cutter (any size you want) stamp out as many large circles as you can get. Using a smaller, round cookie-cutter, stamp out smaller rounds of dough from within the larger rounds to achieve that characteristic ring shape.

Place your ring-shaped donuts and round donut 'centres' on a floured tray and rest for 30 minutes more at room temperature. Preheat the oil in a deep fryer to 180°C. If you don't have a deep fryer, heat 10cm of vegetable oil in a deep pot or saucepan over high heat till it reaches 180°C. When the oil is hot enough, fry the donuts and 'centres' for 2 to 3 minutes, until they turn golden brown. Coat with the white sugar if you'd like to stop here, but why would you when you can dress it up with a heart-stopping glaze?

Here we give you an example of a glaze recipe. To make the maple glaze, mix all ingredients together and beat till smooth. Dip one side of each donut into this glaze and allow it to dry. Load the donuts with more crazy stuff as the glaze dries so that it acts as a 'glue' for these bits and pieces.

CHAPTER
19

Condiments

MAKES
ABOUT
1 ½ CUPS

DUKKA

Dukka is to Egyptians what furikake is to the Japanese. This mix of seeds and nuts is a dynamite Egyptian condiment that's always on our menu in some way or other. You can have it as a dry dip for breads dipped in olive oil, sprinkled liberally over salads and roasted veggies, as a garnish on bean and pulse dishes, or even rubbed unto meat before grilling. Oh and did I mention, it goes great with fried eggs?

Sometimes I like my dukka with pistachios instead of almonds, so feel free to tweak the recipe to your liking. Dukka keeps in an airtight container for up to 2 weeks.

〉〉〉〉〉

3 tbsp coriander seeds, toasted (page 19)
3 tbsp cumin seeds, toasted
8 tbsp white sesame seeds, toasted
50 g almonds, toasted
50 g hazelnuts, toasted
1 tsp sea salt
1 tsp black pepper

Place the toasted coriander and cumin seeds in a pestle and mortar and grind till fine. Add the sesame seeds, almonds and hazelnuts and pound lightly. The final mixture should have a coarse, sandy texture, not something that is too fine and powdery. Season with the salt and pepper, then mix well.

GREEN CHILLI HARISSA

Most people know of red harissa, a fiery chilli paste from North Africa. It's to North Africans what sambal belachan is to us Singaporeans: a multi-purpose hot sauce. At the restaurant, we make a green harissa using green chillies for heat and colour, and a variety of herbs for freshness and flavour. It's one of our all-time favourite condiments, and goes exceptionally well with chicken, lamb, fish and shellfish. Green harissa will keep covered in the fridge for up to 4 weeks.

》》》》》

5 large green chillies, chopped
4 cloves garlic, peeled
½ tsp coriander seeds, toasted
½ cup fresh mint
½ cup fresh coriander
½ cup spring onion, chopped
¼ cup lemon juice
¼ cup water
½ cup sunflower oil
½ tsp salt, plus additional for adjusting

Place all the ingredients into a blender and turn everything into a smoothie. Tip the contents out into a non-stick frying pan and cook over low heat for 8 to 10 minutes, stirring constantly to prevent the bottom of the mix from burning. The final product should be an oily, dark green, extremely fragrant paste. Adjust with more salt to taste if necessary, then allow to cool before serving.

TOUM, THE TOTALLY INSANE GARLIC SAUCE

Toum is the balls—if I could have only one condiment for the rest of my life, this would be it. Slather this Lebanese condiment on a slice of toast for some instant garlic bread. Eat this with fries, fried chicken or roasted lamb. It makes bad cooks look good.

Toum keeps well for up to 1 week in the fridge. Make sure you cover it tightly, unless you like the smell of garlic on everything.

》》》》》

15 cloves garlic, peeled
½ tsp sea salt, plus additional for adjusting
1 egg white
3 tbsp lemon juice, plus additional for adjusting
375 ml sunflower oil
A few cubes of ice

Place all the ingredients, except for the oil and ice, into a blender. Blend on high speed. The garlic will usually fly up the sides of the blender and stick there, so every few seconds, use a rubber spatula to scrape down the garlic. Once the mixture is smooth, leave the motor running and open the hatch in the lid. Trickle in the sunflower oil to form an emulsion. Once the mixture gets too thick and seems to stop blending, add in a cube of ice and blend again. The ice helps to agitate and loosen the mixture, getting it to blend again. Keep alternating between streams of oil and cubes of ice, till all your oil has been incorporated. All this while, continue scraping down the solids from the sides occasionally with your rubber spatula.

Taste the mixture. It will be extremely spicy and pungent at this stage, but that's normal. Season with more salt or lemon juice to your taste. Transfer to a plastic container and keep in the fridge, covered, for 24 hours to let the overly aggressive flavours mellow out. Serve.

CHEATERBUG SMEN

MAKES ABOUT 2 CUPS

No, it's got nothing to do with semen. Smen is a Moroccan fermented butter, traditionally made by storing butter at room temperature for months till it develops a bit of a funky flavour, much like blue cheese. Think of smen as the Moroccan equivalent of MSG, Parmesan cheese or demi-glaze—the element that kicks the umami factor of any dish up a coupla notches. If, like us, you don't have half a year to sit around and wait for your butter to funk itself up, then try our little shortcut.

Use smen to add an insane flavour dimension to stews such as harira (page 133), or sauteed vegetables such as broccoli and mushrooms (page 143).

»»»»

450 g unsalted butter, at room temperature
150 g blue cheese
(such as Gorgonzola Piccante, Roquefort, etc)

Place the butter and blue cheese in a food processor and whiz till well combined.

CHEATERBUG HUMMUS

MAKES ABOUT 3 CUPS

We term this the 'cheaterbug' hummus because canned chickpeas are used instead of freshly cooked ones. Hummus is a Level 101 Middle Eastern dish, as essential to the cuisine as kimchi is to the Koreans. To dress it up a little as a mezze, we sprinkle smoked paprika and sumac on top, throw in a handful of boiled chickpeas tossed with tahini vinaigrette and drizzle olive oil all over. The hummus keeps for 4 days tops in the fridge.

»»»»

2 cups canned chickpeas, drained and washed
½ cup reserved chickpea water from the can
2 cloves garlic, chopped
2 tbsp lemon juice
2 tbsp tahini
2 ice cubes
4 tbsp extra virgin olive oil
Salt
Cold water, for adjusting

Place the chickpeas, chickpea water, garlic, lemon juice, tahini and ice cubes into the bowl of a blender or food processor. Blend for 2 minutes till very smooth. You may have to stop the blending and scrape down the sides of the bowl several times during these 2 minutes. Then, with the motor running, open the hatch in the lid and slowly trickle in the olive oil to form an emulsion. Season well with salt. I like my hummus just firm enough such that it doesn't flow when you tip the plate over. However, if you like your hummus a little runnier, blend a few more spoonfuls of cold water till you're happy with the consistency.

BAHARAT

MAKES ABOUT 1 CUP

SAFFRON MAYO

MAKES ABOUT 2 CUPS

Baharat (which means 'spices' in Arabic) is basically the Middle Eastern equivalent of Chinese five-spice powder. It's a multi-purpose blend of spices that can be used to flavour meats, fish and stews and salads. It keeps well—up to several months—in a cool and dry place.

With our brand of modern Middle Eastern cuisine, we like stringing disparate forms of influence together. Hence, the combination of the Asiatic fragrance of saffron with good ol' mayo. This goes particularly well on top of deep-fried chickpeas (page 177), or simply smeared across a warm pita.

»»»»»

3 tbsp black peppercorns, toasted (page 19)
3 tbsp cumin seeds, toasted
3 tbsp coriander seeds, toasted
1 tbsp cardamon seeds, toasted
   or 1 tbsp ground cardamon
1 tsp cloves, toasted
1 stick cinnamon, about 6 to 8cm long, toasted
2 tsp allspice powder
3 tbsp sweet paprika

»»»»»

5 saffron threads
1 tbsp hot water
1 egg yolk
½ tbsp Dijon mustard
2 cloves garlic, peeled
1 tbsp lemon juice, plus additional for adjusting
1½ cups sunflower oil
A few cubes of ice
Salt

Grind all the spices, except the allspice powder and paprika, into a fine powder in a spice grinder. You may use a mortar and pestle for this, but take note that the cardamom seeds are difficult to grind by hand. You may replace them with ground cardamom. Mix with the allspice powder and paprika. Store in a jar in a cool place.

Place the saffron threads in the hot water and let them 'bloom' for 15 minutes. The water should turn a deep orange colour. Place the egg yolks, mustard, garlic, lemon juice and saffron-water mixture into a blender. Blend on medium speed. With the motor running, open the hatch in the lid and trickle in the sunflower oil to form an emulsion. Once it gets too thick and seems to stop blending, add in a cube of ice and blend again. The ice helps to agitate and loosen the mixture, getting it to blend again. Keep alternating between streams of oil and cubes of ice, till all the oil has been incorporated. Season to taste with salt and more lemon juice.

MECHOUI SPICES

In Morocco, mechoui is a whole sheep or lamb typically roasted in an underground pit. What makes it distinctive is the spice blend. While there are infinite permutations around, here's our simple version.

»»»»
1 part paprika
1 part cumin powder
1 part coriander powder

Simply mix the three spices together.

POMEGRANATE KETCHUP

Served initially as a dip for our Fish Fries (page 99), as we wanted to add a Middle Eastern tinge to common ketchup. Have this with Toum Fries (page 57) too.

»»»»
4 tbsp ketchup
1 tbsp pomegranate molasses
Pinch of sea salt or smoked salt

Simply mix all the ingredients well in a bowl.

POMEGRANATE VINAIGRETTE

Artichoke's house vinaigrette. We splash this on most of our salads for a nice sweet and sour tang.

»»»»
½ clove garlic
½ small shallot
1 tbsp Dijon mustard
3 tbsp pomegranate molasses
3 tbsp lemon juice
1 pinch white sugar
1 pinch sumac (optional, page 17)
1 cup extra virgin olive oil
Salt and pepper

Place all the ingredients except the oil into a blender. Blend on medium speed till smooth. With the motor running, open the hatch in the lid and trickle in the oil to form an emulsion. Season to taste with salt and pepper.

ARTICHOKE-STYLE PICKLES

SMOKED TOMATO EZME

Versatile little buggers. You can serve them alongside any meat or fish dish for a kick of freshness, such as the Artichoke Fried Chicken (page 188) and Quick Butter Bean Ful (page 59). Great in sandwiches too. They will keep in your fridge for up to 3 weeks.

Ezme is basically a Turkish salad made with tomatoes, onions, peppers, fresh herbs and spices, chopped into an amazing scoopable, salsa-like dip. It's typically served as a dip for bread, or a sparkling accompaniment to roast meats and grilled fish. Our version uses smoked paprika for an added dimension of taste, and just because we can.

>>>>>

PICKLING SOLUTION:
½ kg white sugar
1 litre water
1 litre white vinegar
2 cloves
1 bay leaf
1 cinnamon stick (about 2cm long)
1 star anise
1 green cardamom pod
2 pinches of salt

2 carrots, chopped into big matchsticks (about 6cm long)
4 celery stalks, cut into big matchsticks
2 Japanese or Lebanese cucumbers, cut into big matchsticks

To make the pickling solution, place all ingredients into a saucepan and bring to a boil. Once everything is dissolved, remove from heat. Submerge the vegetables in the hot pickling solution and allow to cool in the fridge for 24 hours before serving.

>>>>>

3 large tomatoes, deseeded and finely chopped
½ handful fresh coriander leaves, finely chopped
¼ red onion, finely chopped
1 clove garlic, finely chopped
1 tbsp red pepper paste or tomato paste
1 tbsp clear honey
1 tbsp lemon juice
1 tbsp pomegranate molasses
4 tbsp extra virgin olive oil
Pinch of black pepper
Sea salt
½ tbsp smoked paprika, plus additional for adjusting

Mix all ingredients well in a large mixing bowl. Season generously with sea salt and add more smoked paprika if you like, to boost the smokiness of the ezme. Allow to sit for at least an hour before serving, to allow the flavours to mingle.

Have labneh straight up as a mezze,
drizzled with olive oil and a pinch of za'atar.

LABNEH

MAKES ABOUT 3 CUPS

LABNEH WATER PRANK

SERVES 1 FOOL

Labneh is a strained yoghurt that has the consistency of cream cheese or ricotta. Have it straight up as a mezze, drizzled with olive oil and a pinch of za'atar. Or use it to add richness in dishes—we fold it into our Beetroot Tzatziki (page 80) and dollop it into our meatball sauce (page 27).

We once had a kitchen hand by the name of Ben whom we'd muck around with all the time. He'd always have a glass of iced mocha beside him while he did the dishes as well as his own bottle of cold water in the fridge. Part of his daily routine was to rip off his shirt, roar like a beast and then skull the remaining iced mocha after he'd finish his last round of dishes. Knowing this, the kitchen boys would first replace the water in his water bottle with vinegar, and then they'd slip in some labneh water into his mocha. It never got tiring seeing Ben gag on the labneh-spiked mocha and then attempt to clean his mouth out with a gulp of ice-cold ~~water~~ vinegar.

»»»»

1 kg plain Greek yoghurt
Pinch of salt

»»»»

The funky water that drains out of yoghurt
   as it's hanging in your fridge
An unsuspecting friend's beverage

Mix the yoghurt with the salt, and wrap with a few sheets of cheesecloth. Bundle up the edges of the cheesecloth and tie at the top. Suspend a hook in your fridge and hang the bundle of salted yoghurt for at least 24 hours, with a bowl below to catch the drippings. The longer you hang the yoghurt, the firmer your labneh will be. Sometimes we hang ours for up to 3 days to achieve a very dry, cheese-like texture. Discard the water that drains out of the yoghurt, or use it to punk your friends by spiking their drinks with it (see: Labneh Water Prank).

While your friend isn't looking, add as much labneh water as you can to his drink. Hide around the corner with a video camera and wait for the magic moment when he takes a sip. Serve the video fresh to YouTube.

You can use your labneh immediately or you can roll it into smaller balls and keep them fully submerged under olive oil in the fridge for up to 2 weeks.

Mark gamely demonstrating the results
of the Labneh Water Prank.

LABNEH RANCH DRESSING

MAKES 2 CUPS

ZHOUG

MAKES ABOUT 1 CUP

Ranch dressing is typically made using mayo or yoghurt. To dude up the vast amounts of labneh we have lying around, we decided to put it to good use in ranch dressing. Caraway seeds and onions add another dimension of spice and flavour. Serve it with anything fried, especially cauliflower (page 175).

»»»»

1 cup labneh
1 cup mayonnaise
Caraway seeds, toasted and finely crushed
Coarsely crushed black pepper
Shallots, finely chopped
Chives, finely chopped

The basic foundation of our labneh ranch dressing is a mixture of 1 part labneh to 1 part mayonnaise. With this ratio down pat, you'd have to try really hard to mess it up. From there, mix in as much or as little of caraway seeds, black pepper, shallots, and chives to taste. We like to make ours quite onion-y, so we spam ours with lots of shallots.

Zhoug is a Yemeni chilli-and-garlic sauce that made its way to Israel via the diaspora of Yemenite Jews. Today it's almost ubiquitous in Jewish cuisine, its fiery heat lighting up anything from falafels and shawarma to meats and stews. Zhoug keeps well in the fridge for 3 to 5 days.

»»»»

3 handfuls fresh coriander
3 large green chillies
3 cloves garlic, peeled
1 tsp cumin powder
3 tbsp white wine vinegar
½ tsp sugar
4 tbsp olive oil
½ cup water, plus additional for adjusting
1 tsp salt, plus additional for adjusting

Place all the ingredients in a blender and blend till smooth. Add extra water along the way if the mixture seems to dry; you want to achieve the consistency of a thick smoothie. Season with more salt if necessary.

ROASTED EGGPLANT RELISH

Back in Australia, there was a huge craft aspect to pickling and preserving great produce, especially during the winter months. This eggplant relish is evidence of that influence, even though in Singapore it's easy to get fantastic produce all year round. The vegetal sweetness of eggplant relish is tempered by the tang from balsamic vinegar, making this a superb accompaniment to rich, meaty dishes such as the Lamb Burger (page 76) and Beef and Spinach Brik (page 52). It keeps in the fridge well for 1 to 2 weeks.

»»»»

1 kg's worth of eggplants, coarsely chopped
1 red onion, cut into wedges
4 medium tomatoes
1 tsp coriander seeds, finely crushed
1 tsp cumin seeds, finely crushed
1 cup olive oil, plus additional for frying
Salt and pepper
1 tbsp red pepper paste or tomato paste
1 cup balsamic vinegar
1 cup brown sugar
1 cup water, plus additional for adjusting
1 handful fresh coriander, finely chopped

Preheat your oven to 180°C. Place the eggplants, onion and tomatoes in a large mixing bowl and toss with the coriander seeds, cumin seeds and olive oil. Spread the vegetables out onto a large roasting tray and season well with salt and pepper. Roast the vegetables for 45 minutes, or until they are soft and caramelised.

When the vegetables are ready, put a large saucepan on the stove. Heat up a little more olive oil and fry the roasted onions for a minute over medium heat.

Slip the skins off the tomatoes; they should slide off very easily. Add the tomato flesh to the pan and cook for 1 minute more till it beaks down. Add the red pepper paste and cook for 2 minutes, then add in the balsamic vinegar, brown sugar and water. Bring to a boil and throw in the roasted eggplant. Cook for 10 minutes till everything comes together, adding more water if necessary for moisture. What you're after is a relatively thick, jam-like consistency. Season well with salt and pepper. Remove from heat and stir in the chopped coriander. Place in the fridge and allow to sit overnight before using.

Wanna hold an Artichoke-style party?

Here are some recipe groupings that will make your next brunch/dinner/pig out party a memorable face-stuffing fest…

The bestest, most balls-out and OTT dinner party:

Beetroot Tzatziki with Labneh and Dukka (page 80)

Forgotten Grain Salad (page 81)

Deep-fried Cauliflower with Almonds and Labneh Ranch Dressing (page 175)

Charred Broccoli with Anchovy Sauce and Pickled Garlic (page 213)

The Lambgasm: Artichoke-style Slow-Roasted Lamb Shoulder (page 119)

Artichoke-style Pickles (page 257)

Toum (page 253)

Dessert Smash-up (page 239)

The patriotic dinner party:

Singapore Raw Fish Salad 2013 (page 211)

Bak Chor Mee Sandwich (page 208) / You Tiao Hotdog (page 197) / Bacon Hotdog Pie with Tiger Beer Cheese Soup (page 107) / Char Siew Bao Grilled Cheese Sandwiches (page 110)

The kickass, gut-busting breakfast/brunch party:

Rocket and Sweet Corn Tabbouleh (page 39)

Mushrooms Fried in Smen (page 143)

Butter-whipped Scrambled Eggs (page 194)

Shakshouka with Whatever You Wanna
Put In (page 48)

Smoked Salmon Pancakes with
Bourbon Sour Cream, Wasabi Pea Dukka
and Honey (page 69)

Baklava French Toast with Poached Apricots,
Pistachios and Rose Yoghurt (page 31)

Arabic Lemonade (page 56)

The romantic night in for two:

Roasted Pumpkin with Marmite Honey,
Pumpkin Seed Dukka and Feta (page 125)

Mussels with Merguez Sausage,
Israeli Couscous and Smen (page 45)

Dessert Smash-up (page 239)

The supper club menu for advanced food geeks:

Fried Baby Corn with Avocado Smoothie,
Nuoc Cham and Mint (page 217)

Basturma-style Tuna with Pomelo,
Onions and Roasted Sesame (page 157)

BBQ Calamari with Zhoug, Saffron Mayo
and Rice Krispies (page 109)

Beef Tongue Steaks with Haw Flake Molasses,
Nachos and Braised Cabbage (page 102)

Chermoula BBQ Fish with Preserved
Lemon Butter (page 64)

Smoked Chicken with Pickles and Toum

The casual, easy-to-pull-off dinner party:

Cheaterbug Hummus (page 254)

Basturma and Minted Pea Flatbreads
with Labneh (page 126)

Tzatziki of Local Greens with
Roasted Sesame Seeds (page 146)

Tuna Tartare with Pork Crackling, Ebiko
Labneh and Spicy Nori Cucumber (page 169)

Deep-fried Brussels Sprouts with Honey,
Whipped Feta and Hazelnuts (page 179)

Garlicky Prawns with Ras El Hanout
and Lime (page 30)

The testosterone-filled dudes' night in (McDelivery not allowed):

Mamee Salad with Spam and Egg (page 201)

Fish Fries with Saffron Mayo and
Pomegranate Ketchup (page 99)

Breakfast Smash-up (page 153)

Bacon Sweet Potato Hash with Fried Eggs
and Bourbon Butter (page 161)

Fried Chicken Wings with
Nori Harissa (page 231)

Donuts of Your Wildest Imagination (page 251)

The sweet tooth sleepover:

Grilled Haloumi with Moorish Tomato Salad
and Crispy Vine Leaves (page 145)

Cookie Pie (page 71)

Oreo 'Pancakes' (page 234)

Banana Blueberry Muffin with
Marshmallow Crumble and
Salted Dulce de Leche (page 245)

Turkish Cheaterbug Apple Crumble with
Kataifi Almond Crunch (page 135)

Acknow-
ledgements

I'd like to thank one very important person: my granddad, Sim Miah Kian. Grandpa Sim was the one human being who made Artichoke possible. He was the guy who believed in me when most others thought I was crazy. He's gone home to the Lord, but I'm glad he got to see Artichoke booming during our first four years. Without him, none of this would be here. I also want to thank God for making him my granddad.

Image Credits

Principal photography by Shaun Tan.
Individual photo credits: Wong Maye-E p. 4, 106, 137, 138 (top), 139 (top and bottom), 140, 144, 241, 249; Bjorn Shen p. 12, 23, 28, 32, 34 (headshot), 38, 62, 63, 80, 96, 97, 103, 148, 149, 156, 159, 162, 170, 183 (top right), 202, 205, 206, 207, 210, 214, 250; Jensen Lee p. 24; U.S Government p. 72; Jodin Choo p. 86 (top right); Tim Chew p. 86 (bottom right); Jonathan Lee p. 86 (bottom left); Christine Seah p. 86 (top left); Benedict Quek p. 87 (top left); Joab Immanuel Wong p.87 (second from top left); Anpalagan p. 87 (top right); Tyler Huang p. 87 (bottom right); Jachin Tan p. 87 (bottom left); Loretta Perera p. 95; Glamour Wave Photography, p. 110, 111; www.fotto-graffiti.com, p. 128; Gabriel Chen, p. 40-41, 162, 166-167, 168, 170, 200; Whizarts Wedding Photography, p. 236. **Poster designs:** Stephanie Bui, p. 101, 132, 224, 225.

Index

A

apple, see *Turkish Cheaterbug Apple Crumble*
Arabic Lemonade, 56
Artichoke Fried Chicken, 188
Artichoke-style Pickles, 257
    Artichoke Fried Chicken, 188
    The Lambgasm, 119
    Quick Butter Bean Ful, 59
    Smoked Chicken, 64
avocado,
    Fried Baby Corn with
    Avocado Smoothie, 217
    Open Sandwich of Hummus,
    Dukka and Fried Egg, 33
    Pan-fried Haloumi on Toast, 51

B

beverages,
    Arabic Lemonade, 56
    Chinese New Year Ginger Beer, 155
bacon,
    Bacon Hotdog Pie with
    Tiger Beer Cheese Soup, 107
    Bacon Sweet Potato Hash with
    Fried Eggs and Bourbon Butter, 161
    BLT Fried Rice, 165
    Shakin' Bacon, 163
    baharat, 255,
    Mushrooms Fried in Smen, 143
    Tuna 'Kibbeh Nayeh', 91
Bak Chor Mee Sandwich, 208
Baklava, 246
Baklava French Toast, 31
Banana Blueberry Muffin, 245
basturma,
    Basturma and Minted Pea
    Flatbreads, 126
    Basturma-style Tuna, 157
BBQ Calamari with Zhoug, 109
beef,
    Beef Tongue Steaks with
    Haw Flake Molasses, 102
    Beef, Spinach and Cheese Brik, 52
    Haziz's Super Pimped-up Harira, 133

Meatballs in Spiced Tomato
Sauce, 27
beer,
    Bacon Hotdog Pie with
    Tiger Beer Cheese Soup, 107
    Falafel-battered Fish Nuggets
    with Potato Chip Tabbouleh, 100
Beetroot Tzatziki, 80
BLT Fried Rice, 165
bourbon,
    Bacon Sweet Potato Hash with
    Fried Eggs and Bourbon Butter, 161
    Smoked Salmon Pancakes with
    Bourbon Sour Cream, 69
Breakfast Smash-up, 153
brik, see *Beef, Spinach and Cheese Brik*
broccoli, see *Charred Broccoli with Anchovy Sauce*
Brussels sprouts, see *Deep-fried Brussels Sprouts*
Butter-whipped Scrambled Eggs, 194
bulgur,
    Forgotten Grain Salad, 81
    Rocket and Sweet Corn
    Tabbouleh, 39
    Some Pantry Basics, 17

C

cauliflower, see *Deep-fried Cauliflower*
century egg,
    Ham Chim Peng Burger, 193
    Taiwanese Salt and Pepper
    Pork Ribs, 171
cheese, blue,
    Cheaterbug Smen, 254
cheese, cheddar,
    Bacon Hotdog Pie with
    Tiger Beer Cheese Soup, 107
cheese, cream,
    Ridiculous Cookie Cake, 237
    Smoked Oyster Taramasalata, 43
cheese, feta,
    Roasted Pumpkin with
    Marmite Honey, 125

cheese, haloumi, see *haloumi*
cheese, Manchego,
    Fish Fries, 99
cheese, mascarpone,
    Toasted Semolina Pudding, 90
cheese, melty,
    Beef, Spinach and Cheese Brik, 52
    Fish Fries, 99
cheese, mixed,
    Breakfast Smash-up, 153
    Char Siew Bao Grilled
    Cheese Sandwiches, 110
    Singapore 'Mak & Cheese', 147
chicken,
    Artichoke Fried Chicken, 188
    Crispy Chicken Over Hummus, 131
    Fried Chicken Wings with
    Nori Harissa, 231
    Smoked Chicken, 64
chickpeas, see *Deep-fried Chickpeas*
Char Siew Bao Grilled
Cheese Sandwiches, 110
Charred Broccoli with
Anchovy Sauce, 213
Cheaterbug Hummus, 254,
    Crispy Chicken Over Hummus, 131
    Open Sandwich of Hummus,
    Dukka and Fried Egg, 33
    Pan-fried Haloumi on Toast, 51
Cheaterbug Smen, 254,
    Haziz's Super Pimped-up Harira, 133
    The Lambgasm, 119
    Mushrooms Fried in Smen, 143
    Mussels with Merguez Sausage, 45
    Quick Butter Bean Ful, 59
Chermoula BBQ Fish, 219
Chinese New Year Ginger Beer, 155
condiments,
    Artichoke-style Pickles, 257
    Baharat, 255
    Cheaterbug Hummus, 254
    Cheaterbug Smen, 254
    Dukka, 252
    Green Chilli Harissa, 253
    Labneh, 260
    Labneh Ranch Dressing, 262
    Pomegranate Ketchup, 256

Pomegranate Vinaigrette, 256
Roasted Eggplant Relish, 263
Saffron Mayo, 255
Smoked Tomato Ezme, 257
Toum, 253
Zhoug, 262
cookies,
Cookie Pie, 71
Ridiculous Cookie Cake, 237
Wasabi Pea and Caramelised
White Chocolate Cookies, 248
corn,
Fried Baby Corn with
Avocado Smoothie, 217
Rocket and Sweet Corn
Tabbouleh, 39
crab,
C.R.A.P Sandwich, 227
Crispy Chicken Over Hummus, 131
Crispy Duck Wings, 181

D
Deep-fried Brussels Sprouts, 179
Deep-fried Cauliflower, 175
Deep-fried Chickpeas, 177
desserts,
Baklava, 246
Banana Blueberry Muffin, 245
Cookie Pie, 71
Dessert Smash-up, 239
Donuts of Your Wildest
Imagination, 251
Oreo 'Pancakes', 234
Ridiculous Cookie Cake, 237
Turkish Cheaterbug
Apple Crumble, 135
Wasabi Pea and Caramelised
White Chocolate Cookies, 248
Dessert Smash-up, 239
Donuts of Your Wildest
Imaginations, 251
duck, see Crispy Duck Wings
Dukka, 252,
Beetroot Tzatziki, 80
Open Sandwich of Hummus,
Dukka and Fried Egg, 33

Roasted Pumpkin with
Marmite Honey, 125
Smoked Salmon Pancakes with
Bourbon Sour Cream, 69

E
eggplant,
Beef, Spinach and Cheese Brik, 52
Roasted Eggplant Relish, 263
Turkish-style Eggplant, 83
eggs,
Bacon Sweet Potato Hash with
Fried Eggs and Bourbon Butter, 161
BLT Fried Rice, 165
Breakfast Smash-up, 153
Butter-whipped Scrambled Eggs, 194
Egg mayo (Smoked Salmon Pancakes
with Bourbon Sour Cream), 69
Soft-boiled Quail Eggs, 229
ezme, see Smoked Tomato Ezme

F
fish,
Chermoula BBQ Fish, 219
Falafel-battered Fish Nuggets with
Potato Chip Tabbouleh, 100
Fish 'n Chips with 'Black Tar', 203
Fish and Mussel Chowder, 29
Fish Fries, 99
Singapore Raw Fish Salad 2013, 211
Tuna 'Kibbeh Nayeh', 91
Tuna Tartare with
Pork Crackling, 165
flatbread,
Basturma and Minted Pea
Flatbreads, 126
Crispy Chicken Over Hummus, 131
Quick Butter Bean Ful, 59
Sizzling Prawns with
Green Harissa Cream, 89
Some Pantry Basics, 18
Forgotten Grain Salad, 81
Fried Baby Corn with
Avocado Smoothie, 217
Fried Chicken Wings with
Nori Harissa, 231

fries,
Fish Fries, 99
Toum Fries, 57
ful, see Quick Butter Bean Ful

G
Garlicky Prawns with
Ras El Hanout, 30
Ginger Ale Pork Chops, 154
Green Chilli Harissa, 253,
Sizzling Prawns with
Green Chilli Harissa Cream, 89
Grilled Haloumi Cheese with
Moorish Tomato Salad, 145

H
Hadi's Cold Yoghurt Soup, 42
haloumi,
Grilled Haloumi Cheese with
Moorish Tomato Salad, 145
Pan-fried Haloumi on Toast, 51
Some Pantry Basics, 16
Ham Chim Peng Burger, 193
harira, see Haziz's Super
Pimped-up Harira
Haziz's Super Pimped-up Harira, 133
Harissa-spiced Crab Pate, see C.R.A.P
Sandwich
hotdog, see sausages
hot smoking, 65
hummus, see Cheaterbug Hummus

I
Israeli couscous, see Mussels with
Merguez Sausage

L
labneh, 260:
Basturma and Minted Pea Flatbreads,
126
Beetroot Tzatziki, 80
Meatballs in Spiced
Tomato Sauce, 27
Tuna Tartare with
Pork Crackling, 169

Labneh Ranch Dressing, 262,
Deep-fried Cauliflower, 175
Falafel-battered Fish Nuggets with
Potato Chip Tabbouleh, 100
Forgotten Grain Salad, 81
Lamb Burger, 76
Mamee Salad with
Spam and Egg, 201
Tuna 'Kibbeh Nayeh', 91
Labneh Water Prank, 260
Lamb Burger, 76
lamb,
Lamb Burger, 76
The Lambgasm, 119
Lamb Shoulder Salad, 230
The Lambgasm (Artichoke-style
Slow Roasted Lamb Shoulder), 119
Low, Bjorn, 138-139
Low, Howard and Hui Nan, 63, 64

M

Mamee Salad with
Spam and Egg, 201
Meatballs in Spiced
Tomato Sauce, 27
McNab, Michael, 62, 71
mechoui spices, 256,
Crispy Chicken over Hummus, 131
The Lambgasm, 119
merguez, see Mussels with
Merguez Sausage
mushrooms:
Mushrooms Fried in Smen, 143
Pan-fried Haloumi on Toast, 51
mussels,
Fish and Mussel Chowder, 29
Mussels with Merguez Sausage, 45

N

Nacho 'Hummus' with
Spicy Sausage, 113
nori harissa,
C.R.A.P Sandwich, 227
Fried Chicken Wings with
Nori Harissa, 231
Tuna Tartare with
Pork Crackling, 169

O

Open Sandwich of Hummus,
Dukka and Fried Egg, 33
Oreo 'Pancakes', 234
orange blossom water,
Baklava, 246
Dessert Smash, 239
Ridiculous Cookie Cake, 237
Some Pantry Basics, 17
Overdoughs, 240-244
oyster, see Smoked Oyster
Taramasalata

P

Pan-fried Haloumi on Toast, 51
Pearce, Rob, 138
Pomegranate Ketchup, 256,
Fish Fries, 99
Pomegranate Vinaigrette, 256,
BBQ Calamari with Zhoug, 109, 267
Deep-fried Cauliflower, 175
Forgotten Grain Salad, 81
Mamee Salad with
Spam and Egg, 201
pork,
Bacon Hotdog Pie with
Tiger Beer Cheese Soup, 107
Bacon Sweet Potato Hash with
Fried Eggs and Bourbon Butter, 161
Bak Chor Mee Sandwich, 208
BLT Fried Rice, 165
Char Siew Bao Grilled
Cheese Sandwiches, 110
Ginger Ale Pork Chops, 154
Nacho 'Hummus' with
Spicy Sausage, 113
Shakin' Bacon, 163
Taiwanese Salt and Pepper
Pork Ribs, 171
prawns,
Garlicky Prawns with
Ras El Hanout, 30
Sizzling Prawns with
Green Harissa Cream, 89
pumpkin, see Roasted Pumpkin with
Marmite Honey

Q

Quick Butter Bean Ful, 59

R

Ridiculous Cookie Cake, 237
Roasted Eggplant Relish, 263,
Beef, Spinach and Cheese Brik, 52
Youtiao Hotdog, 197
Lamb Burger, 76
Roasted Pumpkin with
Marmite Honey, 125
Rocket and Sweet Corn
Tabbouleh, 39
Rose + Water + Melon, 232
rosewater,
Baklava French Toast, 31
Some Pantry Basics, 17
Rose + Water + Melon, 232
Roxanne, see Toh, Roxanne

S

Saffron Mayo, 255,
BBQ Calamari with Zhoug, 109
C.R.A.P Sandwich, 227
Deep-fried Chickpeas, 177
Fish Fries, 99
Youtiao Hotdog, 197
salads,
Forgotten Grain Salad, 81
Grilled Haloumi Cheese with
Moorish Tomato Salad, 145
Lamb Shoulder Salad, 230
Mamee Salad with
Spam and Egg, 201
Singapore Raw Fish Salad 2013, 211
sandwiches,
Bak Chor Mee Sandwich, 208
Char Siew Bao Grilled
Cheese Sandwiches, 110
C.R.A.P Sandwich, 227
Open Sandwich of Hummus,
Dukka and Fried Egg, 33
sausages,
Breakfast Smash-up, 153
Bacon Hotdog Pie with
Tiger Beer Cheese Soup, 107
Mussels with Merguez Sausage, 45

Nacho 'Hummus' with
Spicy Sausage, 113
Shakshouka, 48
Youtiao Hotdog, 197
semolina, *see Toasted*
Semolina Pudding
seeds and nuts, *see Toasting*
seeds and nuts
Shakin' Bacon, 163
Shakshouka, 48
Singapore 'Mak & Cheese', 147
Singapore Raw Fish Salad 2013,
211
Sizzling Prawns with
Green Harissa Cream, 89
Smen, *see Cheaterbug Smen*
Smoked Chicken, 64
Smoked Oyster Taramasalata, 43
Smoked Salmon Pancakes with
Bourbon Sour Cream, 69
Smoked Tomato Ezme, 257,
The Lambgasm, 119
Nacho 'Hummus' with
Spicy Sausage, 113
smoking, *see Hot smoking*
Soft-boiled Quail Eggs, 229
sumac,
Falafel-battered Fish Nuggets with
Potato Chip Tabbouleh, 100
Fish Fries, 99
Roasted Pumpkin with
Marmite Honey, 125
Rocket and Sweet Corn
Tabbouleh, 39
Some Pantry Basics, 17

T

tabbouleh,
Falafel-battered Fish Nuggets with
Potato Chip Tabbouleh, 100
Rocket and Sweet Corn
Tabbouleh, 39
tahini,
Artichoke Fried Chicken, 188
Lamb Shoulder Salad, 230
Turkish-style Eggplant, 83

Taiwanese Salt and Pepper
Pork Ribs, 171
Tan, Ming, 63, 69
Toasted Semolina Pudding, 90
toasting seeds and nuts, 19
Toh, Roxanne, 62, 79, 80, 81,
206, 240
Toum, the Totally Insane
Garlic Sauce, 253,
Artichoke Fried Chicken, 188
The Lambgasm, 119
Smoked Chicken, 64
Toum Fries, 57
Youtiao Hotdog, 197
Toum Fries, 57
Tuna 'Kibbeh Nayeh', 91
Tuna Tartare with
Pork Crackling, 169
Turkish Cheaterbug
Apple Crumble, 135
Turkish-style Eggplant, 83
tzatziki,
Beetroot Tzatziki, 80
Tzatziki of Local Greens, 146

W

wasabi peas,
Smoked Salmon Pancakes with
Bourbon Sour Cream, 69
Wasabi Pea and Caramelised
White Chocolate Cookies, 248
watermelon, *see Rose +*
Water + Melon

Y

Yde-Andersen, Henrik, 148
Youtiao Hotdog, 197

Z

za'atar,
Fish and Mussel Chowder, 29
Zhoug, 262
BBQ Calamari with Zhoug, 109
Shakshouka, 48

Stay awesome.